IN SEARCH OF
COLOR EVERYWHERE

A COLLECTION OF
AFRICAN-AMERICAN
POETRY

IN SEARCH OF

Edited by E. Ethelbert Miller

COLOR EVERYWHERE

A COLLECTION OF

Illustrated by Terrance Cummings

AFRICAN-AMERICAN

Stewart, Tabori & Chang NEW YORK

POETRY

FOR MY SON AND DAUGHTER,
NYERE-GIBRAN AND JASMINE-SIMONE

we go into the future
carrying a world
of blackness
yet we have been in the world
and we have gained all of what there
is and was . . .

—AMIRI BARAKA, from "In the Tradition"

Compilation and introduction copyright
© 1994 E. Ethelbert Miller
Illustrations copyright © 1994 Terrance Cummings
Poems copyright © individual poets as noted specifically on
pages 253-256, which constitute an extension of this page.

Published in 1994 and distributed in the U.S.
by Stewart, Tabori & Chang, Inc.
575 Broadway, New York, NY 10012

Distributed in Canada by General Publishing Co. Ltd.,
30 Lesmill Road, Don Mills, Ontario, Canada, M3B 2TX

Distributed in the English language elsewhere in the world
(except Central and South America)
by Melia Publishing Services, P.O. Box 1639,
Maidenhead, Berkshire SL6 6YZ England

Central and South American accounts
should contact Sales Manager, Stewart, Tabori & Chang.

Library of Congress Cataloguing-in-Publication Data
In search of color everywhere: a collection of African-American poetry/
edited by E. Ethelbert Miller: illustrated by Terrance Cummings.
Includes bibliographical reference and indexes.
ISBN 1-55670-339-2
1. American poetry, American—Afro-American authors. 2. Afro-Americans—poetry.
I. Miller, E. Ethelbert.
PS591.N415 1994
811.008'08960773—DC20   94-4395
                                CIP

Book design: Nai Y. Chang and Jim Wageman

Printed in the United States of America
10 9 8 7 6 5 4 3 2 1

INTRODUCTION

In Search of Color Everywhere is a poetic chronicle of the African-American experience and the making of America. Although many poetry collections place contributors in alphabetical and chronological order, *In Search of Color* offers a new structure and format. It presents some of the best poems written by African Americans in a fresh thematic arrangement. The book is divided into seven sections: Freedom; Celebration of Blackness; Love Poems; Family Gatherings; Healing Poems; Rituals: Music, Dance & Sports; and American Journal.

It was easy to find poems about freedom, love, and the celebration of blackness. Freedom has always been a theme found within African-American literature. Among the love poems there are selections that describe heartache and pain. They are combined with poems dedicated to grandmothers and uncles. Many contemporary poets try to write work that rejects the negative images associated with blackness. What one will find in this book are poems that celebrate it but also address the tension of color conflict within the African-American community.

In Search of Color Everywhere is being published during a time when the African-American family is in crisis. Violence, AIDS, child and spouse abuse, divorce, and teen-age pregnancy are all issues we hear about in the media. No family or individual is immune from the crisis; there are no geographical boundaries that offer protection or a safe haven. These problems will not simply disappear and the need to heal and comfort is needed now more than ever. Poetry can help an individual, family, or community cope with grief and suffering.

My major aim in doing this book, however, was to pull together a collection of poems that would make readers laugh and clap their hands. I want people to put this book down and grab a piece of paper just to copy a stanza, maybe post it on the office bulletin board, or keep it on the refrigerator at home—as a reminder. I hope this book will become a family treasure, something to be given from one generation to the next.

Within the pages of this book there is much to ponder. To some the book might seem very political. A lot of the work is nationalistic in tone; no work is anti-white. Instead the poems are pro-black, life giving, and life supporting.

There are references to African-American music in many of the sections. Poems for musicians and about jazz. This book will take you into the church, barber shop, beauty salon, and kitchen, places where African Americans come to laugh, swap stories, and tell their "lies" with joy and fun. We are a warm and loving people when our circle is unbroken.

From Phillis Wheatley to Public Enemy, African-American poets continue to write about the world they see and the world they wish to change. There is a faith in tomorrow, a vision of a better world. There is the resilience of the blues, for we are also, in our blackness, blues people.

Our nation is multicultural, a place of many people in search of a common language. America is a dream as well as an experiment. The last section of the book contains only one poem. It is "[American Journal]," by Robert Hayden. I could think of nothing better to conclude with:

> here among them   the americans   this baffling
> multi people   extremes and variegations   their
> noise   restlessness   their almost frightening
> energy . . .

Out of slavery and bondage African Americans have climbed upwards in search of the mountain top from which a promised land can be seen. Behind us is our legacy, a quilt of song and verse, many voices finding harmony. In Elizabeth Alexander's words:

> " . . . this is your life. Get up and look for color, look for color everywhere."

E. ETHELBERT MILLER
LAS VEGAS, NEVADA
APRIL 18, 1993

CONTENTS

FREEDOM

CELEBRATION OF BLACKNESS

LOVE POEMS

FAMILY GATHERINGS

HEALING POEMS

RITUALS: MUSIC, DANCE & SPORTS

AMERICAN JOURNAL

FREEDOM

THE CREATION
A Negro Sermon

And God stepped out on space,
And He looked around and said,
"I'm lonely
I'll make me a world."

And as far as the eye of God could see
Darkness covered everything,
Blacker than a hundred midnights
Down in a cypress swamp.

Then God smiled,
And the light broke,
And the darkness rolled up on one side,
And the light stood shining on the other,
And God said, *"That's good!"*

Then God reached out and took the light in His hands,
And God rolled the light around in his hands
Until He made the sun;
And He set that sun a-blazing in the heavens.
And the light that was left from making the sun
God gathered it up in a shining ball
And flung it against the darkness,
Spangling the night with the moon and stars.
Then down between
The darkness and the light
He hurled the world;
And God said, *"That's good."*

Then God Himself stepped down —
And the sun was on His right hand
And the moon was on His left;
The stars were clustered about His head,
And the earth was under His feet.
And God walked, and where He trod
His footsteps hollowed the valleys out
And bulged the mountains up.

Then He stopped and looked, and saw
That the earth was hot and barren.
So God stepped over to the edge of the world
And He spat out the seven seas;
He batted His eyes, and the lightnings flashed;
He clapped His hands, and the thunders rolled;
And the waters above the earth came down,
The cooling waters came down.

Then the green grass sprouted,
And the little red flowers blossomed,
The pine tree pointed his finger to the sky,
And the oak spread out his arms,
And the lakes cuddled down in the hollows of the ground,
And the rivers ran to the sea;
And God smiled again,
And the rainbow appeared,
And curled itself around His shoulder.

Then God raised His arm and He waved His hand,
Over the sea and over the land,
And He said, *"Bring forth. Bring forth."*
And quicker than God could drop His hand
Fishes and fowls
And beasts and birds
Swam the rivers and the seas,
Roamed the forests and the woods,
And split the air with their wings.
And God said, *"That's good."*

Then God walked around,
And God looked around
On all that He had made.
He looked at His sun,
And He looked at His moon,
And He looked at His little stars;
He looked on His world,
With all its living things,
And God said, *"I'm lonely still."*

Then God sat down
On the side of a hill where He could think;
By a deep, wide river He sat down;
With His head in His hands,
God thought and thought,
Till He thought, *"I'll make me a man."*

Up from the bed of a river
God scooped the clay;
And by the bank of the river
He kneeled Him down;
And there the great God Almighty
Who lit the sun and fixed it in the sky,
Who flung the stars to the most far corner of the night,
Who rounded the earth in the middle of His hand;
This Great God,
Like a mammy bending over her baby,
Kneeled down in the dust
Toiling over a lump of clay
Till He shaped it in His own image;

Then into it He blew the breath of life,
And man became a living soul.
Amen. Amen.

Once when I was tree
flesh came and worshipped at my roots.
My ancestors slept in my outstretched
limbs and listened to flesh
praying and entreating on his knees.

Once when I was free
African sun woke me up green at dawn.
African wind combed the branches of my hair.
African rain washed my limbs.
African soil nourished my spirit.
African moon watched over me at night.
Once when I was tree
Flesh came to sacrifice at my foot,
Flesh came to preserve my voice,
Flesh came honoring my limbs
as drums, as canoes, as masks,
as cathedrals and temples of the ancestor-gods.

Now flesh comes with metal teeth,
with chopping sticks,
and firelaunchers,
and flesh cuts me down,
and enslaves my limbs to make
forts, ships, pews for other gods,
stockades, flesh pens,
and crosses hung high to sacrifice gods.

Now flesh laughs at my charred and beaten
frame, discarding me in the mud, burning

me up in flames.
Now flesh listens no more to the voice
of the spirits talking through my limbs.

Flesh has grown dull at the ears now.
Flesh has grown pale and lazy.
Flesh has sinned against the fathers.
If flesh would listen I would warn him
that the spirits are displeased
and are planning what to do with him.
But flesh thinks I am dead, charred and gone.

Flesh thinks that by fire he can kill,
thinks that with metal teeth, I die,
thinks that chaining me in alien temples
with new gods carved upon my skin,
thinks that all the voices
linked from root to limb are silenced,
thinks that by cutting me down,
I will sing and dance no more,
but flesh is lazy and clogged with fat.

Flesh does not know that he
did not give me life,
nor can he take it away.

That is what the spirits are singing now.
It is time that flesh
bow down on his knee again!

Phillis Wheatley

ON BEING BROUGHT FROM AFRICA TO AMERICA

Twas mercy brought me from my Pagan land,
Taught my benighted soul to understand
That there's a God, that there's a Saviour too.
Once I redemption neither sought nor knew.
Some view our sable race with scornful eye;
"Their colour is a diabolic dye."
Remember, Christians, Negroes, black as Cain,
May be refined, and join the angelic train.

Frances E. W. Harper

THE SLAVE AUCTION

The sale began — young girls were there,
　Defenceless in their wretchedness,
Whose stifled sobs of deep despair
　Revealed their anguish and distress.

And mothers stood with streaming eyes,
　And saw their dearest children sold;
Unheeded rose their bitter cries,
　While tyrants bartered them for gold.

And woman, with her love and truth —
　For these in sable forms may dwell —
Gazed on the husband of her youth,
　With anguish none may paint or tell.

And men, whose sole crime was their hue,
　The impress of their Maker's hand,
And frail and shrieking children, too,
　Were gathered in that mournful band.

Ye who have laid your love to rest,
　And wept above their lifeless clay,
Know not the anguish of that heart,
　Whose loved are rudely torn away.

Ye may not know how desolate
　Are husbands rudely forced to part,
And how a dull and heavy weight
　Will press the life-drops from the heart.

Robert Hayden

....

RUNAGATE RUNAGATE

1. Runs falls rises stumbles on from darkness into darkness
and the darkness thicketed with shapes of terror
and the hunters pursuing and the hounds pursuing
and the night cold and the night long and the river
to cross and the jack-muh-lanterns beckoning beckoning
and blackness ahead and when shall I reach that somewhere
morning and keep on going and never turn back and keep on going
                    Runagate
                                Runagate
                                        Runagate

Many thousands rise and go
many thousands crossing over

                                        O mythic North
                                O star-shaped yonder Bible city

Some go weeping and some rejoicing
some in coffins and some in carriages
some in silks and some in shackles

                    Rise and go or fare you well

No more auction block for me
no more driver's lash for me

        If you see my Pompey, 30 yrs of age,
        new breeches, plain stockings, negro shoes;
        if you see my Anna, likely young mulatto
        branded E on the right cheek, R on the left,
        catch them if you can and notify subscriber.
        Catch them if you can, but it won't be easy.
        They'll dart underground when you try to catch them,
        plunge into quicksand, whirlpools, mazes,
        turn into scorpions when you try to catch them.

....

And before I'll be a slave
I'll be buried in my grave

North star and bonanza gold
I'm bound for the freedom, freedom-bound
and oh Susyanna don't you cry for me

Runagate

Runagate

11. Rises from their anguish and their power,

Harriet Tubman,

woman of earth, whipscarred,
a summoning, a shining

Mean to be free

And this was the way of it, brethren brethren,
way we journeyed from Can't to Can.
Moon so bright and no place to hide,
the cry up and the patterollers riding,
hound dogs belling in bladed air.
And fear starts a-murbling, Never make it,
we'll never make it. *Hush that now,*
and she's turned upon us, levelled pistol
glinting in the moonlight:
Dead folks can't jaybird-talk, she says;
you keep on going now or die, she says.

Wanted   Harriet Tubman   alias The General
alias Moses   Stealer of Slaves

In league with Garrison   Alcott   Emerson
Garrett   Douglass   Thoreau   John Brown

Armed and known to be Dangerous

Wanted   Reward   Dead or Alive

> Tell me, Ezekiel, oh tell me do you see
> mailed Jehovah coming to deliver me?

Hoot-owl calling in the ghosted air,
five times calling to the hants in the air.
Shadow of a face in the scary leaves,
shadow of a voice in the talking leaves:

> Come ride-a my train

> *Oh that train, ghost-story train*
> *through swamp and savanna movering movering,*
> *over trestles of dew, through caves of the wish,*
> *Midnight Special on a sabre track movering movering,*
> *first stop Mercy and the last Hallelujah.*

> Come ride-a my train

> Mean mean mean to be free.

Robert Hayden

....

FREDERICK DOUGLASS

When it is finally ours, this freedom, this liberty, this beautiful
and terrible thing, needful to man as air,
usable as earth; when it belongs at last to all,
when it is truly instinct, brain matter, diastole, systole,
reflex action; when it is finally won; when it is more
than the gaudy mumbo jumbo of politicians:
this man, this Douglass, this former slave, this Negro
beaten to his knees, exiled, visioning a world
where none is lonely, none hunted, alien,
this man, superb in love and logic, this man
shall be remembered. Oh, not with statues' rhetoric,
not with legends and poems and wreaths of bronze alone,
but with the lives grown out of his life, the lives
fleshing his dream of the beautiful, needful thing.

Elizabeth Alexander

....

PASSAGE

Henry Porter wore good clothes for his journey,
the best his wife could make from leftover
cambric, shoes stolen from the master. They
bit his feet, but if he took them off he feared
he'd never get them on again. He needed

....

to look like a free man when he got there.
Still in a box in the jostling heat,
nostrils to a board pried into a vent,
(a peephole, too, he'd hoped, but there was only
black to see) there was nothing to do
but sleep and dream and weep. Sometimes the dreams
were frantic, frantic loneliness an acid
at his heart. Freedom was near but un-
imaginable. Anxiety roiled inside
of him, a brew which corroded his stomach,
whose fumes clamped his lungs and his throat.
When the salt-pork and cornbread were finished
he dreamed of cream and eggs but the dreams
made him sick. He soiled himself and each time
was ashamed. He invented games, tried to
remember everything his mother
ever told him, every word he hadn't
understood, every vegetable he'd ever
eaten (which was easy: kale, okra, corn,
carrots, beans, chard, yams, dandelion greens),
remember everyone's name who had ever
been taken away. The journey went that way.

When he got there, his suit was chalky
with his salt, and soiled, the shoes waxy with blood.
The air smelled of a surfeit of mackerel.
Too tired to weep, too tired to look through
the peephole and see what freedom looked like,
he waited for the man to whom he'd shipped
himself: Mister William Still, Undertaker,
Philadelphia. He repeated the last
words he'd spoken to anyone: goodbye
wife Clothilde, daughter Eliza,
best friend Luke. Goodbye, everyone, goodbye.
When I can, I'll come for you. I swear,
I'll come for you.

STEAL AWAY

Steal away, steal away, steal away to Jesus,
Steal away, steal away home,
I ain't got long to stay here.

My Lord, He calls me,
He calls me by the thunder,
The trumpet sounds within-a my soul,
I ain't got long to stay here.

Steal away, steal away, steal away to Jesus,
Steal away, steal away home,
I ain't got long to stay here.

Green trees a-bending,
Po' sinner stands a-trembling
The trumpet sounds within-a my soul,
I ain't got long to stay here.

Steal away, steal away, steal away to Jesus,
Steal away, steal away home,
I ain't got long to stay here.

HARRIET TUBMAN AKA MOSES

High in the darkening heavens
    the wind swift, the storm massing
the giant arrow rose, a crackling arch, a sign
    above the fleeing band of people,
toy figures in the canebrake
    below.

Far in the distance, moving quickly,
came the patterrollers
bloodhounds loping, silent.

Minutes before, one of the fleeing band had fallen,
the others for a moment waited
but he did not rise.
A small dark woman stood above him.
His words were slow to come and more a groan:

    Can't make it, just can't make it
    You all go head without me.

Moses pulled out her revolver and she quietly said:

    Move or die.

    You ain't stoppin now
    You *can't* stop now
    You gonna move
    Move or die.

    If you won't go on
    Gonna risk us all —
    Ahma send your soul to glory, I said move!

    Long time now, I got it figgered out
    Ev'ry child a God got a double right, death
    or liberty, Move, now
    or you will die.

....

Listen to me

Way back yonder
    down in bondage
        on my knee
Th' moment that He gave his promise —
I was free

                    (Walk, children)

He said that when destruction rages
He *is* a rock —
    the Rock of Ages
Declared that when the tempest ride
He just come mosey
    straight —
      to my side.

                    (Don't you get weary)

    Promised me the desprit hour
    be the signal for His power
    Hounddogs closin on the track

      Sunlight

and the thunderclap!

                    (How you get weary!)

    Bloodhounds quickenin on the scent
    Over my head, yesss
      the heavens rent!

    O He's a father He *is* a mother
    A sister He will
      be your brother
    Supplies the harvest, He raises up the grain
    O don't you feel — it's fallin now
      the blessed rain.

    Don't make no diffunce if you weary
    Don't mean a hoot owl if you scared
    He was with us in the six troubles
    He won't desert you in the seventh.

Get on up now

That's it, no need a gettin weary
There is a glory there!

There be a great rejoicin
    no more sorrow
    shout 'n *nev*vuh tire
    a great camp meetin
      in that land.

By fire in heaven she was guided
saved by stream
    and by water reed
By her terrible grimace of faith
    beautiful and defiant,
Till, for a moment
    in the long journey
    came the first faint glimpse
    of the stars   the everlasting stars   shining clear
    over the free
          cold
            land.

Dolores Kendrick
....

SIDNEY, LOOKING FOR HER MOTHER . . .

But suh, you've made a mistake. Oh, yes suh! I can't be
    put
on the block no more. I'm free. See. Here be my papers. I
    know I've
got a brand on the back of my neck, as you've noticed, but
    that be from my first
master 'cause I run away too much, but my new master
    gave me my freedom! And

my mistress packed a big basketful of food — more than I
    could eat, enough

for three people! — and gave me money to take the train
    and go to my

freedom and my mother. Oh, my mistress and master be
    good people. Lord

Bless 'em. Now, please let me go 'long. My mother is out
    there somewhere

and you detain me unlawfully. Do you understand the
    papers, suh? Can you

read? No offense, suh. Oh, no! but the train for Austin be
    here any

minute and that be the place where last I heard my mother
    was.

I don't know how strong she be, if all the days of her
    motherhood

be for the mothers of children without mothers, though
    they mothers

be close in they rooms, in they chatters, and in they
    dreams and

playthings, all that motherin' of children, all white and
    fragile,

playin' in the sunlight when the ease of the wind be on
    they faces,

and they hungry cheeks, and they fade sometimes in they
    playing and need

a kiss for they misery. All that motherin' while mothers sip

and sip tea with they kin and talk about the beauty of the
    magnolia or the rose bush

or how expensive they silver be and how much they pay
    for they woman slaves

when they be young and child-bearin' and cheap, and
    sometimes they mother

a horse with tenderness and affection, brush him daily,
    keep him well-fed,

give him a special doctor, and weep when he's ailin', or
    mother

they chatters with friends and mother they fears and
    memories.

I wonder, suh, I don't know, but I wonder if all that
    motherin' which
my mother makes out of clay, sometimes hasn't muted her,
    made her silent,
you know, invisible. But I must go, please suh! I must find
    her and Austin
is where she was last seen, which means her strength be
    there, her visibility,
movin' throughout the land like a moonbeam, takin' care of
    those other than herself.
She be my mother, suh. Do you recognize the sound, if not
    the word? Don't holler,
suh, please don't holler. I'm sick of hollerin', so sick it
    don't scare me
no more. But your throat sounds raspy and must be sore.
    Hollerin' don't help any.

Oh, now! Do you hear it? The train be comin' and I be a
    passenger. The papers,
suh, may I have them back? They simply tell that I'm free,
    can't be put on the
auction block no more. You understand? This man here
    standing next to you can
look at them, if you like, if you give them to him, please,
    suh, quick the train
be. . . . You understand, now? Oh, thank you, suh, thank
    you. I thought you would.
Here be the train. I have one seat and my mother in my
    lap, on my arm, in my
belly, on my tongue, through my eyes. All that and more.
    She out there.
I know it. Gotta get me a seat. And wonder.

FREEDOM

Frances E. W. Harper

BURY ME IN A FREE LAND

Make me a grave where'er you will,
In a lowly plain, or a lofty hill;
Make it among earth's humblest graves,
But not in a land where men are slaves.

I could not rest if around my grave
I heard the steps of a trembling slave;
His shadow above my silent tomb
Would make it a place of fearful gloom.

I could not rest if I heard the tread
Of a coffle gang to the shambles led,
And the mother's shriek of wild despair
Rise like a curse on the trembling air.

I could not sleep if I saw the lash
Drinking her blood at each fearful gash,
And I saw her babes torn from her breast,
Like trembling doves torn from their parent nest.

I'd shudder and start if I heard the bay
Of bloodhounds seizing their human prey,
And I heard the captive plead in vain
As they bound afresh his galling chain.

If I saw young girls from their mothers' arms
Bartered and sold for their youthful charms,
My eye would flash with a mournful flame,
My death-paled cheek grow red with shame.

I would sleep, dear friends, where bloated might
Can rob no man of his dearest right;
My rest shall be calm in any grave
Where none can call his brother a slave.

I ask no monument, proud and high,
To arrest the gaze of the passers-by;
All that my yearning spirit craves,
Is bury me not in a land of slaves.

Spiritual

NO MORE AUCTION BLOCK

No more auction block for me,
No more, no more,
No more auction block for me,
Many thousand gone.

No more peck of corn for me,
No more, no more,
No more peck of corn for me,
Many thousand gone.

No more pint of salt for me,
No more, no more,
No more pint of salt for me,
Many thousand gone.

No more driver's lash for me,
No more, no more,
No more driver's lash for me,
Many thousand gone.

Ahmos Zu-Bolton II

....

STRUGGLE-ROAD DANCE

"when freedom comes
there'll be no more blues

but lawd lawd
it ain't here yet"
— Adesanya Alakoye

This is the camping ground
the waterhole
the rest area

this is the tree
under which I will lay
this poem
      plant it here
      to see if there is growth:

Come to the campfire with me,
make peace with your brothers
love for the sisters,

we make this
a dance of celebration:

      circle the flames
      warm yourself
      and rest . . .

We only wait here
till it dawn on us:

      what is the nature
      of this distance

      how hard was
      that last mile . . .

Count our numbers
(we have never been all present
and accounted for:

      we lost Blackjack
        back at the creek
        bloodriver and some mean nigger
        shooting him down

last we saw of him
he was tiptoeing off into
the white world

at least we think
that's where he
was going . . .

But Livewire Davis
made it, and Sister Blue
survived —

this place
must be a workshop
for our people

make a home
and build a family

study
the growth
of our tribe

we know how far off
is morning

      when freedom comes
      there'll be no more blues

(this dance
will not be sung
when sweet freedom dawns on us
but

      sing it now
      sing it now
      sing it now

Jean Toomer

SONG OF THE SON

Pour O pour that parting soul in song,
O pour it in the sawdust glow of night,
Into the velvet pine-smoke air to-night,
And let the valley carry it along.
And let the valley carry it along.

O land and soil, red soil and sweet-gum tree,
So scant of grass, so profligate of pines,
Now just before an epoch's sun declines
Thy son, in time, I have returned to thee,
Thy son, I have in time returned to thee.

In time, for though the sun is setting on
A song-lit race of slaves, it has not set;
Though late, O soil, it is not too late yet
To catch thy plaintive soul, leaving, soon gone,
Leaving, to catch thy plaintive soul soon gone.

O Negro slaves, dark purple ripened plums,
Squeezed and bursting in the pine-wood air,
Passing, before they stripped the old tree bare
One plum was saved for me, one seed becomes

An everlasting song, a singing tree,
Caroling softly souls of slavery,
What they were, and what they are to me,
Caroling softly souls of slavery.

Traditional

TAKE THIS HAMMER

Take this hammer — huh!
And carry it to the captain — huh!
You tell him I'm gone — huh!
Tell him I'm gone — huh!

If he asks you — huh!
Was I runnin' — huh!
You tell him I was flyin' — huh!
Tell him I was flyin' — huh!

If he asks you — huh!
Was I laughin' — huh!
You tell him I was cryin' — huh!
You tell him I was cryin' — huh!

Sharyn Jeanne Skeeter

MIDWEST, MIDCENTURY

Put up a windmill on
this flat land

took sod and built a home
made a clearing
for our tired feet

through with running
we bought horses
from the widow in town
blond hair covered her eyes
she spit when we rode away

there is no hiding here
no trees, no caves
with our black faces
open to the sun
we work the fields
plant wheat for ourselves

Sharyn Jeanne Skeeter
....

CALIFORNIA, 1852

This earth gave us
nothing but granite and oak
I am not rich

last month when my
shovel broke, me
and Mexican Joe
got some pans
went down to the river
at dawn
green moss slimey
on rocks
shining in water
no gold

I am free
I am a mountain lion
without a deer
hungry I go
to the mine

boss man clean
against the pines
in soft leather shoes
and tall hat
pays us with vinegar pie
and red beans
I dig gold from cliffs
its weight like iron
chains pulls
tight around my chest

Sharyn Jeanne Skeeter
....

WESTERN TRAIL COOK, 1880

Mostly, the men
want buffalo steak
and soda bread
tea cakes are too
sweet for trappers'
blood when they come
to my cabin whiskey
drunk, they call me
Old Sarah and lasso
my skirts

Tom, my man, died
on a rope in Missouri
I followed cattle
herds to Texas
Baby died of fever
dug dry earth out back
with my raw hands
covered his body
with brown rocks
and tumbleweed

Monkey John called
me a lady
fried me prairie dog
with bacon
unbuttoned my
checkered dress
left me a room
of tobacco smoke

Sonia Sanchez

....

RIGHT ON: WHITE AMERICA

this country might have
been a pio
              neer land
once.
    but.   there ain't
no mo
          indians   blowing
custer's mind
              with a different
image of america.
                              this country
might have
              needed shoot/
outs/ daily/
              once.
                    but. there ain't
no mo real/ white/   allamerican
                              bad/guys.
just.
      u & me.
                blk/ and un/armed.
this country might have
been a pion
              eer land.   once.
                                        and it still is.
check out
            the falling
gun/shells   on our blk/tomorrows.

Claude McKay

·········

THE WHITE HOUSE

Your door is shut against my tightened face,
And I am sharp as steel with discontent;
But I possess the courage and the grace
To bear my anger proudly and unbent.
The pavement slabs burn loose beneath my feet,
A chafing savage, down the decent street;
And passion rends my vitals as I pass,
Where boldly shines your shuttered door of glass.
Oh, I must search for wisdom every hour,
Deep in my wrathful bosom sore and raw,
And find in it the superhuman power
To hold me to the letter of your law!
Oh, I must keep my heart inviolate
Against the potent poison of your hate.

Primus St. John

·········

LYNCHING AND BURNING

Men lean toward the wood.
Hoods crease
Until they find people
Where there used to be hoods.
Instead of a story,
The whole thing becomes a scream
        then time, place, far,
        late in the country,
        alone,
        an old man's farm.
Children we used to call charcoal,
Now they smell that way — deliberately,
And the moon stares at smoke like iced tea.

Daughter,
        Once there was a place we called the earth.
        People lived there. Now we live there . . .

BETWEEN THE WORLD AND ME

And one morning while in the woods I stumbled suddenly upon the thing,
Stumbled upon it in a grassy clearing guarded by scaly oaks and elms.
And the sooty details of the scene rose, thrusting themselves between the world
    and me. . . .

There was a design of white bones slumbering forgottenly upon a cushion of ashes.
There was a charred stump of a sapling pointing a blunt finger accusingly at the sky.
There were torn tree limbs, tiny veins of burnt leaves, and a scorched coil of greasy
    hemp;
A vacant shoe, an empty tie, a ripped shirt, a lonely hat, and a pair of trousers stiff
    with black blood.
And upon the trampled grass were buttons, dead matches, butt-ends of cigars and
    cigarettes, peanut shells, a drained gin-flask, and a whore's lipstick;
Scattered traces of tar, restless arrays of feathers, and the lingering smell of gasoline.
And through the morning air the sun poured yellow surprise into the eye sockets of
    a stony skull. . . .
And while I stood my mind was frozen with a cold pity for the life that was gone.
The ground gripped my feet and my heart was circled by icy walls of fear —
The sun died in the sky; a night wind muttered in the grass and fumbled the leaves
    in the trees; the woods poured forth the hungry yelping of hounds; the darkness
    screamed with thirsty voices; and the witnesses rose and lived:
The dry bones stirred, rattled, lifted, melting themselves into my bones.
The grey ashes formed flesh firm and black, entering into my flesh.
The gin-flask passed from mouth to mouth; cigars and cigarettes glowed, the whore
    smeared the lipstick red upon her lips,
And a thousand faces swirled around me, clamoring that my life be burned. . . .

And then they had me, stripped me, battering my teeth into my throat till I
    swallowed my own blood.
My voice was drowned in the roar of their voices, and my black wet body slipped
    and rolled in their hands as they bound me to the sapling.
And my skin clung to the bubbling hot tar, falling from me in limp patches.
And the down and quills of the white feathers sank into my raw flesh, and I
    moaned in my agony.
Then my blood was cooled mercifully, cooled by a baptism of gasoline.
And in a blaze of red I leaped to the sky as pain rose like water, boiling my limbs.
Panting, begging I clutched childlike, clutched to the hot sides of death.
Now I am dry bones and my face a stony skull staring in yellow surprise at the
    sun. . . .

AN OLD WOMAN REMEMBERS

Her eyes were gentle; her voice was for soft singing
In the stiff-backed pew, or on the porch when evening
Comes slowly over Atlanta. But she remembered.

She said: "After they cleaned out the saloons and the dives
The drunks and the loafers, they thought that they had better
Clean out the rest of us. And it was awful.
They snatched men off of street-cars, beat up women.
Some of our men fought back, and killed too. Still
It wasn't their habit. And then the orders came
For the milishy, and the mob went home,
And dressed up in their soldiers' uniforms,
And rushed back shooting just as wild as ever.
Some leaders told us to keep faith in the law,
In the governor; some did not keep that faith,
Some never had it: he was white too, and the time
Was near election, and the rebs were mad.
He wasn't stopping hornets with his head bare.
The white folks at the big houses, some of them
Kept all their servants home under protection
But that was all the trouble they could stand.
And some were put out when their cooks and yard-boys
Were thrown from cars and beaten, and came late or not at all.
And the police they helped the mob, and the milishy
They helped the police. And it got worse and worse.

"They broke into groceries, drug-stores, barber shops,
It made no difference whether white or black.
They beat a lame bootblack until he died,
They cut an old man open with jack-knives
The newspapers named us black brutes and mad dogs,
So they used a gun butt on the president
Of our seminary where a lot of folks
Had sat up praying prayers the whole night through.

"And then," she said, "our folks got sick and tired
Of being chased and beaten and shot down.
All of a sudden, one day, they all got sick and tired.
The servants they put down their mops and pans,
And brooms and hoes and rakes and coachman whips,
Bad niggers stopped their drinking Dago red,
Good Negroes figured they had prayed enough,
All came back home — they'd been too long away —
A lot of visitors had been looking for them.

"They sat on their front stoops and in their yards,
Not talking much, but ready; their welcome ready:
Their shotguns oiled and loaded on their knees.

"And then
There wasn't any riot any more."

Claude McKay
....

IF WE MUST DIE

If we must die, let it not be like hogs
Hunted and penned in an inglorious spot,
While round us bark the mad and hungry dogs,
Making their mock at our accursèd lot.
If we must die, O let us nobly die,
So that our precious blood may not be shed
In vain; then even the monsters we defy
Shall be constrained to honor us though dead!
O kinsmen! we must meet the common foe!
Though far outnumbered let us show us brave,
And for their thousand blows deal one death-
    blow!
What though before us lies the open grave?
Like men we'll face the murderous, cowardly
    pack,
Pressed to the wall, dying, but fighting back!

E. Ethelbert Miller
·········

TOMORROW

tomorrow
i will take the
journey back
sail
the
middle passage

it
would be better
to be packed
like spoons again
than
to continue to
live among
knives and forks

Sterling A. Brown

·········

STRONG MEN

The strong men keep coming on.
— Sandburg

They dragged you from the homeland,
They chained you in coffles,
They huddled you spoon-fashion in filthy hatches,
They sold you to give a few gentlemen ease.

They broke you in like oxen,
    They scourged you,
    They branded you,
    They made your women breeders,
    They swelled your numbers with bastards . . . . .
    They taught you the religion they disgraced.
    You sang:
            Keep a-inchin' along
            Lak a po' inch worm . . .
    You sang:
            By and bye
            I'm gonna lay down this heaby load . . .
    You sang:
            Walk togedder, chillen,
            Dontcha git weary . . .
                The strong men keep a-comin' on
                The strong men get stronger.

They point with pride to the roads you built for them,
    They ride in comfort over the rails you laid for them.
    They put hammers in your hands
    And said — Drive so much before sundown.
    You sang:
            Ain't no hammah
            In dis lan'
            Strikes lak mine, bebby,
            Strikes lak mine.
They cooped you in their kitchens,
    They penned you in their factories,
    They gave you the jobs that they were too good for,
    They tried to guarantee happiness to themselves
    By shunting dirt and misery to you.

....
You sang:

        Me an' muh baby gonna shine, shine
        Me an' muh baby gonna shine.
           The strong men keep a-comin' on
           The strong men git stronger . . .

They bought off some of your leaders
    You stumbled, as blind men will . . .
    They coaxed you, unwontedly soft-voiced . . .
    You followed a way.
    Then laughed as usual.
    They heard the laugh and wondered;
    Uncomfortable;
    Unadmitting a deeper terror . . .
           The strong men keep a-comin' on
           Gittin' stronger . . .

    What, from the slums
    Where they have hemmed you,
    What, from the tiny huts
    They could not keep from you —
    What reaches them
    Making them ill at ease, fearful?
    Today they shout prohibition at you
    "Thou shalt not this"
    "Thou shalt not that"
    "Reserved for whites only"
    You laugh.

One thing they cannot prohibit —

        The strong men . . . coming on
        The strong men gittin' stronger.
        Strong men . . .
        Stronger . . .

June Jordan

....

POEM ABOUT MY RIGHTS

Even tonight and I need to take a walk and clear
my head about this poem about why I can't
go out without changing my clothes my shoes
my body posture my gender identity my age
my status as a woman alone in the evening/
alone on the streets/alone not being the point/
the point being that I can't do what I want
to do with my own body because I am the wrong
sex the wrong age the wrong skin and
suppose it was not here in the city but down on the beach/
or far into the woods and I wanted to go
there by myself thinking about God/or thinking
about children or thinking about the world/all of it
disclosed by the stars and the silence:
I could not go and I could not think and I could not
stay there
alone
as I need to be
alone because I can't do what I want to do with my own
body and
who in the hell set things up
like this
and in France they say if the guy penetrates
but does not ejaculate then he did not rape me
and if after stabbing him if after screams if
after begging the bastard and if even after smashing
a hammer to his head if even after that if he
and his buddies fuck me after that
then I consented and there was
no rape because finally you understand finally
they fucked me over because I was wrong I was
wrong again to be me being me where I was/wrong
to be who I am
which is exactly like South Africa
penetrating into Namibia penetrating into
Angola and does that mean I mean how do you know if
Pretoria ejaculates what will the evidence look like the
proof of the monster jackboot ejaculation on Blackland
and if

after Namibia and if after Angola and if after Zimbabwe
and if after all of my kinsmen and women resist even to
self-immolation of the villages and if after that
we lose nevertheless what will the big boys say will they
claim my consent:
Do You Follow Me: We are the wrong people of
the wrong skin on the wrong continent and what
in the hell is everybody being reasonable about
and according to the *Times* this week
back in 1966 the c.i.a. decided that they had this problem
and the problem was a man named Nkrumah so they
killed him and before that it was Patrice Lumumba
and before that it was my father on the campus
of my Ivy League school and my father afraid
to walk into the cafeteria because he said he
was wrong the wrong age the wrong skin the wrong
gender identity and he was paying my tuition and
before that
it was my father saying I was wrong saying that
I should have been a boy because he wanted one/a
boy and that I should have been lighter skinned and
that I should have had straighter hair and that
I should not be so boy crazy but instead I should
just be one/a boy and before that
it was my mother pleading plastic surgery for
my nose and braces for my teeth and telling me
to let the books loose to let them loose in other
words
I am very familiar with the problems of the c.i.a.
and the problems of South Africa and the problems
of Exxon Corporation and the problems of white
America in general and the problems of the teachers
and the preachers and the f.b.i. and the social
workers and my particular Mom and Dad/I am very
familiar with the problems because the problems
turn out to be
me
I am the history of rape
I am the history of the rejection of who I am
I am the history of the terrorized incarceration of
my self

I am the history of battery assault and limitless
armies against whatever I want to do with my mind
and my body and my soul and
whether it's about walking out at night
or whether it's about the love that I feel or
whether it's about the sanctity of my vagina or
the sanctity of my national boundaries
or the sanctity of my leaders or the sanctity
of each and every desire
that I know from my personal and idiosyncratic
and indisputably single and singular heart
I have been raped
be-
cause I have been wrong the wrong sex the wrong age
the wrong skin the wrong nose the wrong hair the
wrong need the wrong dream the wrong geographic
the wrong sartorial I
I have been the meaning of rape
I have been the problem everyone seeks to
eliminate by forced
penetration with or without the evidence of slime and/
but let this be unmistakable this poem
is not consent I do not consent
to my mother to my father to the teachers to
the F.B.I. to South Africa to Bedford-Stuy
to Park Avenue to American Airlines to the hardon
idlers on the corners to the sneaky creeps in
cars
I am not wrong: Wrong is not my name
My name is my own my own my own
and I can't tell you who the hell set things up like this
but I can tell you that from now on my resistance
my simple and daily and nightly self-determination
may very well cost you your life

BETWEEN OURSELVES

Once when I walked into a room
my eyes would seek out the one or two black faces
for contact or reassurance or just a sign
I was not alone.
Now walking into rooms of black faces
who would destroy me for any difference
to whom shall my eyes look?
Once it was much easier to know
who were my people.

Yet if we were stripped of all our pretenses
and our flesh was cut away
the sun would bleach all our bones
as white
as the face of my black mother
was bleached white by gold
or Orishala
and how does that measure me?

I do not believe
our wants have made all our lies
holy.

Under the sun on the shores of Elmina
a black man sold the woman who carried
my grandmother in her belly
he was paid with coins of a bright yellow
that shone in the evening sun
and in the faces of her sons and daughters.
When I see that brother behind my eyes
his irises are bloodless and without color
his tongue clicks like the yellow coins
tossed up on this shore
where we share the same corner of an alien and corrupted heaven
and whenever I try to eat the words
of easy blackness as salvation
I taste the color of my grandmother's first betrayal.

2.   But I do not whistle his name at the shrine of Shopona
bringing down the juices of death upon him
nor forget Orishala, called god of whiteness
who works in the dark wombs of night
forming the shapes we all wear
so that even cripples and dwarfs and albinos
are sacred worshippers when the boiled corn is offered.
Humility lies in the face of history.
I have forgiven myself for him
for the white meat we all consumed in secret
before we were born
we shared the same meal.

When you impale me upon your lances
of narrow blackness
without listening to my heart speak
mourn your own borrowed blood, your own borrowed visions.
Do not mistake my flesh for the enemy
do not write my name in the dust
before the shrine of the god of smallpox
for we are all children of Eshu
god of chance and the unpredictable
and we each wear many changes inside our skin.

Now armed by old scars that have healed
in many different colours
I look into my own faces
as Eshu's daughter crying
if we do not stop killing the other
in ourselves
the self that we hate
in others
soon we shall all lie
in the same direction
and Eshidale's priests will be very busy
who alone must bury
all those who seek their own death
by jumping up from the ground
and landing upon their heads.

Gil Scott-Heron

·········

WINTER IN AMERICA

From the Indians who welcomed the pilgrims
to the buffalo who once ruled the plains;
like the vultures circling beneath the dark clouds
looking for the rain/looking for the rain.
From the cities that stagger on the coast lines
in a nation that just can't take much more/
like the forest buried beneath the highways
never had a chance to grow/never had a chance
    to grow.
It's winter; winter in america
and all of the healers have been killed or forced
    away.
It's winter; winter in america
and ain't nobody fighting 'cause nobody knows
    what to save.
The con-stitution was a noble piece of paper;
with Free Society they struggled but they died in
    vain/
and now Democracy is ragtime on the corner
hoping that it rains/hoping that it rains.
And I've seen the robins perched in barren
    treetops
watching last ditch racists marching across the
    floor
and like the peace signs that melted in our
    dreams
never had a chance to grow/never had a
    chance to grow.
it's winter; winter in america
and all of the healers done been killed or put in
    jail
it's winter, winter in america
and ain't nobody fighting 'cause nobody knows
    what to save.

it is so hard to be earth bound
when yr wings are aching to challenge the high-tide
of a revolutionary wind.
so hard to remain terrestrial when the skin remembers
being bird. and the heart soars back and forth in its
ribbed cage . . .
the song of the crow gives rebirth to a loneliness that
manifests itself in the flight-time of the life-time.
it is so hard to be earthbound
wings dragging beside u on the ground
u cld lift them if folks wld just get off of 'em.
they kno u're dependable so they lean on u
hopin to be included on yr next flight.
and not being able to take off gives u the woes
occasionally u claw at what loves u the most
and everything u sing after that is beyond even the blues.

so much is lost when the lost claim to be the only thing
happenin. they eat, sleep, and excrete in fear of being genetically
assassinated. the unsurpassed splendor of our united plumage makes
them plot to slaughter the bird in us. their media tells us to hate the sky.
they make us think that stagnation is better than flight of any kind,
motion of any sort. they trick us into turning in our wings. and they burn

the wings that are not turned in.

but sometimes, the way we can feel about each otha is totally
regenerating to the most scorched wings.

the right look, an opening smile that never closes,
sometimes, the way we dare to feel about each otha, is
all the flight-times of the most magnificent birds in all
the worlds where luv and freedom are a way of being.
sometimes, we do that to each otha.

wanna fly?

Lucille Clifton
....

I AM ACCUSED OF TENDING TO THE PAST

i am accused of tending to the past
as if i made it,
as if i sculpted it
with my own hands. i did not.
this past was waiting for me
when i came,
a monstrous unnamed baby,
and i with my mother's itch
took it to breast
and named it
History.
she is more human now,
learning language everyday,
remembering faces, names and dates.
when she is strong enough to travel
on her own, beware, she will.

Michelle Parkerson

STATISTIC

In 1944
the lives of black boys
were worth nothing
and you were
no stranger to bloodshed
or the drives of men
in a Southern sawmill town

That carolina dawn
came tender
and 2 white girls
raped and murdered
led to a black boy's door

You were 14
no stranger to bloodshed
or the drives of men

In newspaper photos
eyes caved with wisdom
lips without question
a child resigned
to a man's fate

In 1944
the lives of black boys
were worth nothing
and George Stinney, Jr.
was given the chair

The youngest face
on Death Row
was dark
silent

Now the sons
he never fathered
learn his lesson well:
You are black and male
in america
You are never
too young to die

Etheridge Knight

TO MAKE A POEM IN PRISON

It is hard
To make a poem in prison.
The air lends itself not
to the singer.
The seasons creep by unseen
And spark no fresh fires.

Soft words are rare, and drunk drunk
Against the clang of keys;
Wide eyes stare fat zeros
And plea only for pity.

Pity is not for the poet;
Yet poems must be primed.
Here is not even sadness for singing,
Not even a beautiful rage rage,
No birds are winging. The air
Is empty of laughter. And love?
Why, love has flown,
Love has gone to glitten.

June Jordan

....

POEM AGAINST THE STATE (OF THINGS): 1975

wherever I go (these
days)
the tide seems low
(oh) wherever I go (these
days)
the tide seems very
very low

ATTICA!
ALLENDE!
AMERIKA!

Welcome to the Sunday School
of outfront machineguns
and secretive
assassinations

EVERYBODY WELCOME!

Put your money on the plate
your feet on the floor
and better keep a bodyguard
standing at the open door

EVERYBODY WELCOME!

Almighty
Multinational
Corporate
Incorporeal
Bank of the World
The World Bank
Diplomacy
            and Gold

This is the story:
This is the prayer:

            Rain fell
            Monday the thirteenth
            1971
            Attica

....
coldstone covered by a cold moon-
light hidden by the night
when fifteen hundred Black
Puerto Rican
White (one or two)
altogether Fifteen Hundred Men
plus
thirty-eight hostages
(former keepers of the keys
to the ugliest
big
house of them all)
Fifteen Hundred and Thirty
Eight
Men
lay sleeping in a long
wait
for the sun
and not one with a gun
not one with a gun

(oh) wherever I go
the tide seems low

Fifteen Hundred and Thirty
Eight
prisoners in prison
at Attica/they
lay sleeping in a long
long wait
for the sun
and not one with a gun
not one with a gun

But they were not really alone:

ATTICA!
ALLENDE!
AMERIKA!

....
Despite
the quiet of the cold moon-
light on the coldstone
of the place
Despite
the rain that fell
transforming the D-yard
blankets and tents
into heavyweight, soggy
and sweltering hell

The Brothers were hardly alone:

on the roofs
on the walkways
in turrets
and tunnels
from windows
and whirlybirds

overhead

The State
Lay in wait

Attica Attack Troops
wearing masks
carrying gas cannisters
and proud to be white
proud to be doing
what everyone can
for The Man
Attica Attack Troops
lay armed
at the ready
legalized killers
hard
chewing gum
to master an all-American impatience
to kill

....
to spill blood
to spill blood of the Bloods

and not one with a gun

the State
lay in wait

Attica Attack Troops
carrying pistols and
big-game/.270 rifles and
Ithaca Model 37 shotguns
with double-o buckshot
and also
shotguns appropriate
for "antivehicle duty"
or shotguns appropriate
for "reducing a cement block wall
to rubble"
they were ready

for what?

(oh) wherever I go (these
days)
the tide seems low

Fifteen Hundred and Thirty Eight
Prisoners
lay waiting for the next
day's sun
Fifteen Hundred and Thirty Eight
Brothers
asleep
and not one with a gun
not one with a gun

....

II   Why did the Brothers revolt
against Attica?

why were they there?

What did they want?

the minimum wage
less pork
fresh fruit
religious freedom
and more than one shower a week

What did they want?

a response
recognition
as men
"WE are MEN!" They
 declared:
"WE are MEN!
 We are not beasts and do not
 intend to be beaten
 or driven as such."

ATTICA!
ALLENDE!
AMERIKA!

The State
lay in wait.

III   *Black woman weeping at the coldstone wall*
Rain stops. And blood begins to fall

"JACKPOT ONE!" was the animal
cry of The State
in its final
reply
 "JACKPOT ONE!!"
was the cry

9:26 A.M.
Monday the thirteenth
September, 1971
Police
State Troopers
prison guards
helicopters/The Attica Attack Troops
terrified the morning
broke through
to the beasts within them
beasts
unleashed by the Almighty
Multinational
Corporate
Incorporeal
Bank of the World
Despoilers
of Harlem
Cambodia
Chile
Detroit
the Philippines
Oakland
Montgomery
Dallas
South Africa
Albany
Attica
Attica
The Attica Killers
The Almighty State shot/
murdered/massacred
forty three men
forty three men

....
The other Brothers/they
were gassed and
beaten
bleeding or not
still clubbed and beaten:

"Nigger! You should
  have got it through the head!
  Nigger! You gone wish that you were
  dead!   Nigger!   Nigger!"

Monday the Thirteenth
September, 1971
Attica
Blood fell on the Brothers: Not one with a gun.
Black women weeping into coldstone.

IV   *wherever I go (these*
                      days)
                      the tide seems low
                      (oh) wherever I go (these
                       days)
                       the tide seems very
                       very low

                      God's love has turned away
                      from this Almighty place
                      But
                      I will pray
                      one prayer while He yet grants me
                      time and space:

                      NO MORE AND NEVER AGAIN!
                      NO MORE AND NEVER AGAIN!

                      A-men.
                      A-men.
                                        1975

FOR MY PEOPLE

For my people everywhere singing their slave songs
      repeatedly: their dirges and their ditties and their blues
      and jubilees, praying their prayers nightly to an
      unknown god, bending their knees humbly to an unseen
      power;
For my people lending their strength to the years: to the
      gone years and the now years and the maybe years,
      washing ironing cooking scrubbing sewing mending
      hoeing plowing digging planting pruning patching
      dragging along never gaining never reaping never
      knowing and never understanding;
For my playmates in the clay and dust and sand of Alabama
      backyards playing baptizing and preaching, and doctor
      and jail and soldier and school and mama and
      cooking and playhouse and concert and store and
      Miss Choomby and hair and company;
For the cramped bewildered years we went to school to
      learn to know the reasons why and the answers to and
      the people who and the places where and the days
      when, in memory of the bitter hours when we discovered
      we were black and poor and small and different
      and nobody wondered and nobody understood;
For the boys and girls who grew in spite of these things to
      be Man and Woman, to laugh and dance and sing and
      play and drink their wine and religion and success, to
      marry their playmates and bear children and then die
      of consumption and anemia and lynching;
For my people thronging 47th Street in Chicago and Lenox
      Avenue in New York and Rampart Street in New
      Orleans, lost disinherited dispossessed and HAPPY people
      filling the cabarets and taverns and other people's
      pockets needing bread and shoes and milk and land
      and money and Something — Something all our own;
For my people walking blindly, spreading joy, losing time
      being lazy, sleeping when hungry, shouting when burdened,
      drinking when hopeless, tied and shackled and
      tangled among ourselves by the unseen creatures who
      tower over us omnisciently and laugh;

For my people blundering and groping and floundering in
　　the dark of churches and schools and clubs and
　　societies, associations and councils and committees and
　　conventions, distressed and disturbed and deceived
　　and devoured by money-hungry glory-craving leeches,
　　preyed on by facile force of state and fad and novelty
　　by false prophet and holy believer;
For my people standing staring trying to fashion a better
　　way from confusion from hypocrisy and misunderstanding,
　　trying to fashion a world that will hold all
　　the people all the faces all the adams and eves and
　　their countless generations;
Let a new earth rise. Let another world be born. Let a bloody
　　peace be written in the sky. Let a second generation
　　full of courage issue forth, let a people loving freedom
　　come to growth, let a beauty full of healing and a
　　strength of final clenching be the pulsing in our spirits
　　and our blood. Let the martial songs be written, let
　　the dirges disappear. Let a race of men now rise and
　　take control!

Public Enemy
(Ridenhour/Shocklee/Sadler)
....

PARTY FOR YOUR RIGHT TO FIGHT

Power Equality
And we're out to get it
I know some of you ain't wit'it
This party started right in '66
With a pro-word Black radical mix
Then at the hour of twelve
Some force cut the power
And emerged from hell
It was your so called government
That made this occur
Like the grafted devils they were

J. Edgar Hoover, and he coulda' proved to 'ya
He had King and X set up
Also the party with Newton, Cleaver and Seale
He ended—so get up

Time to get 'em back—You got it
Get back on the track—You got it
Word from the honorable Elijah Muhammed
Know who you are to be Black

To those that disagree, it causes static
For the original Black Asiatic man
Cream of the earth
And was here first
And some devils prevent this from being known
But you check out the books they own
Even masons they know it
But refuse to show it—Yo
But it's proven and fact
And it takes a nation of millions to hold us back

LIFT EVERY VOICE AND SING

Lift every voice and sing
Till earth and heaven ring,
Ring with the harmonies of Liberty;
Let our rejoicing rise
High as the listening skies,
Let it resound loud as the rolling sea.
Sing a song full of the faith that the dark past has taught us,
Sing a song full of the hope that the present has brought us,
Facing the rising sun of our new day begun
Let us march on till victory is won.

Stony the road we trod,
Bitter the chastening rod,
Felt in the days when hope unborn had died;
Yet with a steady beat,
Have not our weary feet
Come to the place for which our fathers sighed?
We have come over a way that with tears have been watered,
We have come, treading our path through the blood of the slaughtered,
Out from the gloomy past,
Till now we stand at last
Where the white gleam of our bright star is cast.

God of our weary years,
God of our silent tears,
Thou who has brought us thus far on the way;
Thou who has by Thy might
Led us into the light,
Keep us forever in the path, we pray.
Lest our feet stray from the places, Our God, where we met Thee,
Lest, our hearts drunk with the wine of the world, we forget Thee;
Shadowed beneath Thy hand,
May we forever stand.
True to our GOD,
True to our native land.

Mari Evans

·········

WHO CAN BE BORN BLACK

Who
can be born black
and not
sing
the wonder of it
the joy
the
challenge

And/to come together
in a coming togetherness
vibrating with the fires of pure knowing
reeling with power
ringing with the sound above sound above sound
to explode/in the majesty of our oneness
our comingtogether
in a comingtogetherness

Who
can be born
black
and not exult!

Lance Jeffers

·········

MY BLACKNESS IS THE BEAUTY OF THIS LAND

My blackness is the beauty of this land,
my blackness,
tender and strong, wounded and wise,
my blackness:
I, drawling black grandmother, smile muscular and sweet,
unstraightened white hair soon to grow in earth,
work-thickened hand thoughtful and gentle on grandson's
                    head,
my heart is bloody-razored by a million memories' thrall:

remembering the crook-necked cracker who spat
     on my naked body,
remembering the splintering of my son's spirit
     because he remembered to be proud
remembering the tragic eyes in my daughter's
     dark face when she learned her color's
     meaning,

and my own dark rage a rusty knife with teeth to gnaw
     my bowels,
my agony ripped loose by anguished shouts in Sunday's
     humble church,
my agony rainbowed to ecstasy when my feet oversoared
     Montgomery's slime,

ah, this hurt, this hate, this ecstasy before I die,
and all my love a strong cathedral!
My blackness is the beauty of this land!

Lay this against my whiteness, this land!
Lay me, young Brutus stamping hard on the cat's tail,
gutting the Indian, gouging the nigger,
booting Little Rock's Minniejean Brown in the buttocks and
     boast,
     my sharp white teeth derision-bared as I the
     conqueror crush!
Skyscraper-I, white hands burying God's human clouds
     beneath the dust!
Skyscraper-I, slim blond young Empire
     thrusting up my loveless bayonet to rape the sky,
then shrink all my long body with filth and in the gutter lie
as lie I will to perfume this armpit garbage,
While I here standing black beside
wrench tears from which the lies would suck the salt
to make me more American than America . . .
But yet my love and yet my hate shall civilize this land,
this land's salvation.

Langston Hughes

DREAM VARIATION

To fling my arms wide
In some place of the sun,
To whirl and to dance
Till the white day is done.
Then rest at cool evening
Beneath a tall tree
While night comes on gently,
    Dark like me —
That is my dream!

To fling my arms wide
In the face of the sun,
Dance! Whirl! Whirl!
Till the quick day is done.
Rest at pale evening . . .
A tall, slim tree . . .
Night coming tenderly
    Black like me.

Langston Hughes

THE NEGRO SPEAKS OF RIVERS
(to W. E. B. Du Bois)

I've known rivers:
I've known rivers ancient as the world and older than the
    flow of human blood in human veins.

My soul has grown deep like the rivers.

I bathed in the Euphrates when dawns were young.
I built my hut near the Congo and it lulled me to sleep.
I looked upon the Nile and raised the pyramids above it.
I heard the singing of the Mississippi when Abe Lincoln
    went down to New Orleans, and I've seen its muddy
    bosom turn all golden in the sunset.

I've known rivers:
Ancient, dusky rivers.

My soul has grown deep like the rivers.

William Edward Burghardt Du Bois

....

THE SONG OF THE SMOKE

I am the smoke king,
I am black.
I am swinging in the sky.
I am ringing worlds on high:
I am the thought of the throbbing mills,
I am the soul of the soul toil kills,
I am the ripple of trading rills,

Up I'm curling from the sod,
I am whirling home to God.
I am the smoke king,
I am black.

I am the smoke king,
I am black.
I am wreathing broken hearts,
I am sheathing devils' darts;
Dark inspiration of iron times,
Wedding the toil of toiling climes
Shedding the blood of bloodless crimes,

Down I lower in the blue,
Up I tower toward the true,
I am the smoke king,
I am black.

I am the smoke king,
I am black.

I am darkening with song,
I am hearkening to wrong;
I will be black as blackness can,
The blacker the mantle the mightier the man,
My purpl'ing midnights no day dawn may ban.

I am carving God in night,
I am painting hell in white.
I am the smoke king,
I am black.

I am the smoke king,
I am black.

I am cursing ruddy morn,
I am nursing hearts unborn;
Souls unto me are as mists in the night,
I whiten my blackmen, I beckon my white,
What's the hue of a hide to a man in his might!
Hail, then, grilly, grimy hands,

Sweet Christ, pity toiling lands!
Hail to the smoke king,
Hail to the black!

Bob Kaufman

....

UNTITLED

THE SUN IS A NEGRO.
THE MOTHER OF THE SUN IS A NEGRO.
THE DISCIPLES OF THE
SUN ARE NEGRO.
THE SAINTS OF THE
SUN ARE NEGRO.
HEAVEN IS NEGRO.

Nikki Giovanni

EGO TRIPPING
(there may be a reason why)

I was born in the congo
I walked to the fertile crescent and built
    the sphinx
I designed a pyramid so tough that a star
       that only glows every one hundred years falls
       into the center giving divine perfect light
I am bad

I sat on the throne
       drinking nectar with allah
I got hot and sent an ice age to europe
       to cool my thirst
My oldest daughter is nefertiti
       the tears from my birth pains
       created the nile
I am a beautiful woman

I gazed on the forest and burned
       out the sahara desert
       with a packet of goat's meat
       and a change of clothes
I crossed it in two hours
I am a gazelle so swift
       so swift you can't catch me

       For a birthday present when he was three
I gave my son hannibal an elephant
       He gave me rome for mother's day
My strength flows ever on

My son noah built new/ark and
I stood proudly at the helm
       as we sailed on a soft summer day
I turned myself into myself and was
       jesus

men intone my loving name
All praises All praises
I am the one who would save

I sowed diamonds in my back yard
My bowels deliver uranium
    the filings from my fingernails are
    semi-precious jewels
    On a trip north
I caught a cold and blew
My nose giving oil to the arab world
I am so hip even my errors are correct
I sailed west to reach east and had to round off
    the earth as I went
    The hair from my head thinned and gold was laid
    across three continents

I am so perfect so divine so ethereal so surreal
I cannot be comprehended
    except by my permission

I mean . . . I . . . can fly
    like a bird in the sky . . .

Maya Angelou

·········

STILL I RISE

You may write me down in history
With your bitter, twisted lies,
You may trod me in the very dirt
But still, like dust, I'll rise.

Does my sassiness upset you?
Why are you beset with gloom?
'Cause I walk like I've got oil wells
Pumping in my living room.

Just like moons and like suns,
With the certainty of tides,
Just like hopes springing high,
Still I'll rise.

Did you want to see me broken?
Bowed head and lowered eyes?
Shoulders falling down like teardrops,
Weakened by my soulful cries.

Does my haughtiness offend you?
Don't you take it awful hard
'Cause I laugh like I've got gold mines
Diggin' in my own back yard.

You may shoot me with your words,
You may cut me with your eyes,
You may kill me with your hatefulness,
But still, like air, I'll rise.

Does my sexiness upset you?
Does it come as a surprise
That I dance like I've got diamonds
At the meeting of my thighs?

Out of the huts of history's shame
I rise
Up from a past that's rooted in pain
I rise
I'm a black ocean, leaping and wide,
Welling and swelling I bear in the tide.
Leaving behind nights of terror and fear
I rise
Into a daybreak that's wondrously clear
I rise
Bringing the gifts that my ancestors gave,
I am the dream and the hope of the slave.
I rise
I rise
I rise.

Elouise Loftin

....

WEEKSVILLE WOMEN

"Old women will not enter Paradise:
they will be made young and beautiful first." — The Prophet

old Black ladies
carryin shopping bags
full of more shopping bags
memories and dreams
gap their legs
on buses
and say things like
"dont God work in mysterious ways, baby
sweety, yours is just startin, sugar"
old Black ladies with wise written
on their faces   youth&future
written in their eyes
spread wide open up to me
stretch out their feet
cast down on their legs
and adjust their veins
like road maps   they say
where they got on   when they got to leave
and fan fan fan
they got so much
to be hot about

Langston Hughes

....

MOTHER TO SON

Well, son, I'll tell you:
Life for me ain't been no crystal stair.
It's had tacks in it,
And splinters,
And boards torn up,
And places with no carpet on the floor —
Bare.
But all the time
I'se been a-climbin' on,
And reachin' landin's,
And turnin' corners,
And sometimes goin' in the dark
Where there ain't been no light.
So boy, don't you turn back.
Don't you set down on the steps
'Cause you finds it's kinder hard.
Don't you fall now —
For I'se still goin', honey,
I'se still climbin',
And life for me ain't been no crystal stair.

Melvin E. Brown

....

SURVIVAL MOTION: NOTICE

We gotta   america's
put more in our   got all kinds of
children's heads   attractive distractive
than gold   colorful
teeth,   freak image
to   clown clothed
keep   hypnotic animal
blackness   music games
to   and rides.
keep
blackness   and you
to   can lose a child
always   at a circus,
keep   very
it   easy.
from
turning around.

Carolyn Rodgers

....

POEM NO. 1

our faces are the
light & dark window panes
we paint our smiles on.
behind them,
we hide the vulnerabilities
we want no one else to see.
the water colors of our tears,
even, the rainbows of our laughter . . .
and the heart that can look
through to another heart
might turn away from the face,
        but heart to heart
            as face to face should be
are eyes, that need not hide.

ILLUSION

I hate wide mouth black girls
with their loud walnut faces.
I hate their bright white eyes
and evil tongues,

their hen cackle laughs
that startle birds
roosting in trees miles away.
I hate their graceful jungle steps,
the steps they fall into too easily,
a downbeat only they can hear.

They stir cities,
cause concrete to tremble.
I hate the way their backs
taper into a narrow base
before spreading, graceful
round and proud as a peacock's.

Their firm black legs
insult me with swift movements,
feet in tempo even as they walk
to pick up the evening paper;
turning pages noisily to find
comic strips, the rustle of paper
paced with the pop of many sticks
of Juicy Fruit.

I hate the popping fingers,
the soft flash of color
turning like butterscotch buds
in a field of wind wild
dandelion greens.

I turn away from high cheek bones
and wide spread mocha nostrils
finely honed to catch the scent
of paddy-rollers or pig faced sheriffs.

This country has made them
sassyfaced.
They sneer at mousey mongoloid blondes
who move coolly blind
through a forest of suburbs,
lisping about posh uptown hotels.

I hate the pain that makes them
bulldog their way through
downtown crowds,
makes them nurture dead minds
and naturally accent cheap clothes
with finely curved licorice colored shoulders.

They bury Nefertiti charms
under outstretched lips,
grow older under frowns
and a hurricane of bad manners;

they grow barbed, cold,
these Sapphires and Mabel Sues
from ebony to dusky brown,
from creme and rust to lemon yellow.

They are my sisters
and we sit in a barracks of noise,
trading screams with wandering
no-caring   louder   brothers.

Akasha (Gloria) Hull
....
ANOTHER RHYTHM

Little girl   turning pain
grown up   to peace

Little grown-up girl   Rise up now
                       woman
We've cried   Adorn yourself
We've held ourselves
We've rocked   Let your light
to the rhythm   and beauty
of tears   shine

Paul Laurence Dunbar
....
WE WEAR THE MASK

We wear the mask that grins and lies,
It hides our cheeks and shades our eyes, —
This debt we pay to human guile;
With torn and bleeding hearts we smile,
And mouth with myriad subtleties.

Why should the world be over-wise,
In counting all our tears and sighs?
Nay, let them only see us, while
    We wear the mask.

We smile, but, O great Christ, our cries
To thee from tortured souls arise.
We sing, but oh the clay is vile
Beneath our feet, and long the mile;
But let the world dream otherwise,
    We wear the mask.

Weldon J. Irvine, Jr.
··········

TO BE YOUNG, GIFTED, AND BLACK

Young, gifted, and black
Oh what a lovely precious dream.
To be young, gifted, and black
Open your heart to what I mean.
In the whole world you know
There's a million boys and girls
Who are young, gifted, and black
And that's a fact!

You are young, gifted, and black
We must begin to tell our young,
"There's a world waiting for you.
Yours is the quest that's just begun.
When you're feeling real low
There's a great truth that you should know
When you're young, gifted, and black
Your soul's intact!"

Ah to be young, gifted, and black
Oh how I've longed to know the truth.
There are times when I look back
And I am haunted by my youth.
But my joy of today
Is that we can all be proud to say,
"To be young, gifted, and black
Is where it's at! Is where it's at! Is where it's **at!"**

Toi Derricotte
....

A NOTE ON MY SON'S FACE

1. Tonight, I look, thunderstruck
   at the gold head of my grandchild.
   Almost asleep, he buries his feet
   between my thighs;
   his little straw eyes
   close in the near dark.
   I smell the warmth of his raw
   slightly foul breath, the new death
   waiting to rot inside him.
   Our breaths equalize our heartbeats;
   every muscle of the chest uncoils,
   the arm bones loosen in the nest
   of nerves. I think of the peace
   of walking through the house,
   pointing to the name of this, the name of that,
   an educator of a new man.

   Mother.   Grandmother.   Wise
   Snake-woman who will show the way;
   Spider-woman whose black tentacles
   hold him precious. Or will tear off his head,
   her teeth over the little husband,
   the small fist clotted in trust at her breast.

   This morning, looking at the face of his father,
   I remembered how, an infant, his face was too dark,
   nose too broad, mouth too wide.
   I did not look in that mirror
   and see the face that could save me
   from my own darkness.
   Did he, looking in my eye, see
   what I turned from:
   my own dark grandmother
   bending over gladioli in the field,
   her shaking black hand defenseless
   at the shining cock of flower?

   I wanted that face to die,
   to be reborn in the face of a white child.

I wanted the soul to stay the same,
for I loved to death,
to damnation and God-death,
the soul that broke out of me.
I crowed: My Son!   My Beautiful!
But when I peeked in the basket,
I saw the face of a black man.

Did I bend over his nose
and straighten it with my fingers
like a vine growing the wrong way?
Did he feel my hand in malice?

Generations we prayed and fucked
for this light child,
the shining god of the second coming;
we bow down in shame
and carry the children of the past
in our wallets, begging forgiveness.

II. A picture in a book,
a lynching.
The bland faces of men
who watch Christ go up in flames, smiling,
as if he were a hooked
fish, a felled antelope, some
wild thing tied to boards and burned.
His charring body
gives off light — a halo
burns out of him.
His face scorched featureless;
the hair matted to the scalp
like feathers.
His head flops back, looking up,
as if his last words were a blessing.
One man stands with his hand on his hip,
another with his arm
slung around the shoulder of a friend,
as if this moment were large enough
to hold affection.

Waring Cuney
....
NO IMAGES

She does not know
Her beauty,
She thinks her brown body
Has no glory.

If she could dance
Naked,
Under palm trees
And see her image in the river
She would know.

But there are no palm trees
On the street,
And dishwater gives back no
images.

William J. Harris
....
A DADDY POEM

My father is a hand-
some guy.

Looks like
a cross between
Clark Gable & Ernest Hemingway.
If you don't believe me,
I got proof:
Once a white woman
(at one of those
          parties)
said, to my father,
"You're good looking
for a colored man."

Nancy Travis
....
SUNBATHING

trying so hard
to be white
we got darker

naked blond head
dolls do not
dangle under these arms. tea
cups half filled
with imaginary tea
are no longer
being passed to
imaginary friends.

i have cut
the long monotonous
connection between
me and my blue
diary.

i use to hate
babies
and bottles, being
married. becoming
twenty-six
(too close to thirty).

use to use noxema, artra
setting lotion
with pink cushion rollers
that popped
a loose
at night.
this mind
has stopped
its noon
day fights.

it is
peaceful here.

i smile
in the mirror
at my wide
ass/spaghetti
thin legs.

i have no doubts
of who
i am, i am
a believer
in myself!

i have learned
to love
this crazy
reddish brown
girl.
i am stretching
releasing
retrieving.
i can laugh
out loud
show my gap
and be pleased
with the distance
i've traveled.

Wanda Coleman

....

COFFEE

steam rises over my nose
against this night
cold empty room as wide as my throat; eases/flows
river a mocha memory from aunt ora's
kitchen. she made it in the
big tin percolator and poured the brew into thick
white fist-sized mugs and
put lots of sugar and milk in it for me and
the other kids who loved it better than chocolate
and the neighbor woman used to tell her and us
it wasn't good for young colored children
to drink. it made you get blacker
and blacker

Harriet Jacobs

....

ON GROWING UP THE DARKER BERRY

there were rules
like the man had to be darker
than the woman, her lightness making her
more desirable   more a flower
to his earth and i wanted so
to be a flower

Dudley Randall

BLACKBERRY SWEET

Black girl black girl
lips as curved as cherries
full as grape bunches
sweet as blackberries

Black girl black girl
when you walk you are
magic as a rising bird
or a falling star

Black girl black girl
what's your spell to make
the heart in my breast
jump   stop   shake

Sonia Sanchez

TO ANITA

high/yellow/black/girl
walken like the sun u be.
move on even higher.
                        those who
laugh at yo/color
                    have not moved
to the blackness we be about
cuz as Curtis Mayfield be sayen
we people be darker than blue
                        and quite a few
of us be yellow
                all soul/shades of
blackness.
            yeah. high/yellow/black/girl
        walk yo/black/song
            cuz some of us
                be hearen yo/sweet/**music.**

Charlotte Watson Sherman

....

ROOTS

I am sorry you are
proud of the man
who raped your
great-great-great
grandmother and left
your hair good.
Please, this is not
envy it is sorrow
for the long road
we must travel
to be sisters. My
lineage can be traced
through the roots
of my hair to
Nairobi. Do not
try to make me
ashamed of this
fact, sorry my hair
grows in dry tight
cottonfields on my
head and will not
fly in the wind
like the woman I am not.

Alvin Aubert

....

THE OPPOSITE OF GREEN

the blonde neighbor lady tells my wife
looking square past her dark skin
into her deep black eyes,

"i can't make a thing grow.
i even kill weeds.
i have a black thumb."

Mari Evans

....

I AM A BLACK WOMAN

I am a black woman
the music of my song
some sweet arpeggio of tears
is written in a minor key
and I
can be heard humming in the night
Can be heard
                    humming
in the night

I saw my mate leap screaming to the sea
and I/with these hands/cupped the lifebreath
from my issue in the canebrake
I lost Nat's swinging body in a rain of tears
and heard my son scream all the way from Anzio
for Peace he never knew. . . . I
learned Da Nang and Pork Chop Hill
in anguish
Now my nostrils know the gas
and these trigger tire/d fingers
seek the softness in my warrior's beard

I
am a black woman
tall as a cypress
strong
beyond all definition still
defying place
and time
and circumstance
    assailed
        impervious
            indestructible
Look
    on me and be
renewed

Audre Lorde

....

NATURALLY

Since Naturally Black is Naturally Beautiful
I must be proud
And, naturally
Black and
Beautiful
Who always was a trifle
Yellow
And plain, though proud,
Before.

Now I've given up pomades
Having spent the summer sunning
And feeling naturally free
   (if I die of skin cancer
   oh well — one less
   black and beautiful me)
Yet no agency spends millions
To prevent my summer tanning
And who trembles nightly
With the fear of their lily cities being swallowed
By a summer ocean of naturally woolly hair?

But I've bought my can of
Natural Hair Spray
Made and marketed in Watts
Still thinking more
Proud beautiful Black women
Could better make and use
Black bread.

BLACK WOMAN

My hair is springy like the forest grasses
that cushion the feet of squirrels —
crinkled and blown in a south breeze
like the small leaves of native bushes.

My black eyes are coals burning
like a low, full jungle moon
through the darkness of being.
In a clear pool I see my face,
know my knowing.

My hands move pianissimo
over the music of the night:
gentle birds fluttering through leaves and grasses
they have not always loved,
nesting, finding home.

Where are my lovers?
Where are my tall, my lovely princes
dancing in slow grace
toward knowledge of my beauty?
Where
are my beautiful
black men?

Maya Angelou

. . . .

PHENOMENAL WOMAN

Pretty women wonder where my secret lies.
I'm not cute or built to suit a fashion model's size
But when I start to tell them,
They think I'm telling lies.
I say,
It's in the reach of my arms,
The span of my hips,
The stride of my step,
The curl of my lips.
I'm a woman
Phenomenally.
Phenomenal woman,
That's me.

I walk into a room
Just as cool as you please,
And to a man,
The fellows stand or
Fall down on their knees.
Then they swarm around me,
A hive of honey bees.
I say,
It's the fire in my eyes,
And the flash of my teeth,
The swing in my waist,
And the joy in my feet.
I'm a woman
Phenomenally.
Phenomenal woman,
That's me.

Men themselves have wondered
What they see in me.
They try so much
But they can't touch
My inner mystery.
When I try to show them
They say they still can't see.
I say,
It's in the arch of my back,
The sun of my smile,
The ride of my breasts,
The grace of my style.
I'm a woman
Phenomenally.
Phenomenal woman,
That's me.

Now you understand
Just why my head's not bowed.
I don't shout or jump about
Or have to talk real loud.
When you see me passing
It ought to make you proud.
I say,
It's in the click of my heels,
The bend of my hair,
The palm of my hand,
The need for my care.
'Cause I'm a woman
Phenomenally.
Phenomenal woman,
That's me.

Blackness
is a title,
is a preoccupation,
is a commitment Blacks
are to comprehend —
and in which you are
to perceive your glory.

The conscious shout
of all that is white is
"It's Great to be white."
The conscious shout
of the slack in Black is
"It's Great to be white."
Thus all that is white
has white strength and yours.

The word Black
has geographic power,
pulls everybody in:
Blacks here —
Blacks there —
Blacks wherever they may be.
And remember, you Blacks, what they told you —
remember your Education:
    "one Drop — one Drop
maketh a brand new Black."
            Oh mighty Drop.
            —— And because they have given us kindly
so many more of our people

Blackness
stretches over the land.
Blackness —
the Black of it,
the rust-red of it,
the milk and cream of it,
the tan and yellow-tan of it,
the deep-brown middle-brown high-brown of it,
the "olive" and ochre of it —
Blackness
marches on.

The huge, the pungent object of our prime out-ride
is to Comprehend,
to salute and to Love the fact that we are Black,
which *is* our "ultimate Reality,"
which is the lone ground
from which our meaningful metamorphosis,
from which our prosperous staccato,
group or individual, can rise.

Self-shriveled Blacks.
Begin with gaunt and marvelous concession:
YOU are our costume and our fundamental bone.

     All of you —
     you COLORED ones,
     you NEGRO ones,
those of you who proudly cry
     "I'm half INDian" —
     those of you who proudly screech
     "I've got the blood of George Washington in
        MY veins —"

ALL of you —
     you proper Blacks,
you half-Blacks,
you wish-I-weren't Blacks,
Niggeroes and Niggerenes.

You.

James Brown and Alfred Ellis

....

SAY IT LOUD — I'M BLACK AND I'M PROUD

Say it loud, I'm black and I'm proud
Say it loud, I'm black and I'm proud
Some people say we got a lot of malice
Some say it's a lot of nerve
But I say we won't quit moving
Until we get what we deserve
We've been 'buked and we've been scorned
We've been treated bad, talked about as sure as you're born
But just as sure as it takes two eyes to make a pair
Brother we can't quit until we get our share.

Whoee — out of sight tomorrow night — it's tough
You're tough enough — whoee — it's hurting me
Say it loud, I'm black and I'm proud
Say it loud, I'm black and I'm proud
Say it loud, I'm black and I'm proud.

I've worked on jobs with my feet and my hands
But all that work I did was for the other man
Now we demand a chance to do things for ourselves
We're tired of beating our head against the wall
And working for someone else
We're people, we're like the birds and the bees
But we'd rather die on our feet than keep living on our knees.

Lance Jeffers

....

WHEN I KNOW THE POWER OF MY BLACK HAND

I do not know the power of my hand,
I do not know the power of my black hand.

I sit slumped in the conviction that I am powerless,
tolerate ceilings that make me bend.
My godly mind stoops, my ambition is crippled;
I do not know the power of my hand.

I see my children stunted,
my young men slaughtered,
I do not know the mighty power of my hand.

I see the power over my life and death in
another man's hands, and sometimes
I shake my woolly head and wonder:

   Lord have mercy! What would it be like . . . to be free?

But when I know the mighty power of my black hand
   I will snatch my freedom from the tyrant's mouth,
know the first taste of freedom on my eager tongue,
sing the miracle of freedom with all the force
   of my lungs,
christen my black land with exuberant creation,
stand independent in the hall of nations,
root submission and dependence from the soil of my soul
and pitch the monument of slavery from my back when
I know the mighty power of my hand!

Lucille Clifton
....

LISTEN CHILDREN

listen children
keep this in the place
you have for keeping
always
keep it all ways

we have never hated black

listen
we have been ashamed
hopeless   tired   mad
but always
  all ways
we loved us

we have always loved each other
children   all   ways

pass it on

LOVE POEMS

DESIRE 1.

i have been all my lovers
i have been better than my lovers
i have been those better than i
the ones i've never met
the ones i've met and never got
their secret side things
the ones i imagine
i have been my desires
i have been loved
in moments i have loved myself
having love is the key to having love
it is as simple as they ever said
i have been with people
i have been more than with people
i have been amongst myself
there is alone as well
and without self
these are even often better
my self cannot be imagined
i cannot seriously imagine you
but it has never mattered
i enjoy you/all ways

SONG IN SPITE OF MYSELF

Never love with all your heart,
 It only ends in aching;
And bit by bit to the smallest part
 That organ will be breaking.

Never love with all your mind,
 It only ends in fretting;
In musing on sweet joys behind,
 Too poignant for forgetting.

Never love with all your soul,
 For such there is no ending,
Though a mind that frets may find control,
 And a shattered heart find mending.

Give but a grain of the heart's rich seed,
 Confine some under cover,
And when love goes, bid him God-speed.
 And find another lover.

Rita Dove
....

ADOLESCENCE—I

In water-heavy nights behind grandmother's porch
We knelt in the tickling grasses and whispered:
Linda's face hung before us, pale as a pecan,
And it grew wise as she said:
        "A boy's lips are soft,
         As soft as baby's skin."
The air closed over her words.
A firefly whirred near my ear, and in the distance
I could hear streetlamps ping
Into miniature suns
Against a feathery sky.

Rita Dove
....

ADOLESCENCE—II

Although it is night, I sit in the bathroom, waiting.
Sweat prickles behind my knees, the baby-breasts are alert.
Venetian blinds slice up the moon; the tiles quiver in pale strips.

Then they come, the three seal men with eyes as round
As dinner plates and eyelashes like sharpened tines.
They bring the scent of licorice. One sits in the washbowl,

One on the bathtub edge; one leans against the door.
"Can you feel it yet?" they whisper.
I don't know what to say, again. They chuckle,

Patting their sleek bodies with their hands.
"Well, maybe next time." And they rise,
Glittering like pools of ink under moonlight,

And vanish. I clutch at the ragged holes
They leave behind, here at the edge of darkness.
Night rests like a ball of fur on my tongue.

ADOLESCENCE—III

With Dad gone, Mom and I worked
The dusky rows of tomatoes.
As they glowed orange in sunlight
And rotted in shadow, I too
Grew orange and softer, swelling out
Starched cotton slips.

The texture of twilight made me think of
Lengths of Dotted Swiss. In my room
I wrapped scarred knees in dresses
That once went to big-band dances;
I baptized my earlobes with rosewater.
Along the window-sill, the lipstick stubs
Glittered in their steel shells.

Looking out at the rows of clay
And chicken manure, I dreamed how it would happen:
He would meet me by the blue spruce,
A carnation over his heart, saying,
"I have come for you, Madam;
I have loved you in my dreams."
At his touch, the scabs would fall away.
Over his shoulder, I see my father coming toward us:
He carries his tears in a bowl,
And blood hangs in the pine-soaked air.

SLAVE RITUAL

when I asked him about
                it
he said he had to do
                   that.
had to
      knock her down, slap her,
beat her up, chastise her . . .
how else
would she know
he loved her?

she understood
it wasn't nothing serious
nothing, "personal"
    she'd get up knowing
    she was going down again
she never would hold the floor
and wait out the count,
somehow
that would have been unfair,
not part
        of it. . . .

she never even imagined
               packing her
bags and
leaving him.
what you leave a good man fuh?

he paid the rent, went to work everyday
bought groceries,
occasionally.
why, where would she go?
and to who? who would
love her better? any "differently"
she knew he would never
kill her
she seldom had a bruise,
that showed . . .
just a knock here & now
a slap there & then
to ease the pain of
      BEING
together. . . .

once, I knocked on their door
and asked if I could help
They BOTH became angry at me
"Go home stupid! Don't you have any of your
      own business to mine?"
Sometimes when my neighbors are not
       fighting
they talk to me
They Say,
THEY LOVE EACH OTHER.

Askia M. Toure

THE FRONTIER OF RAGE

The frontier of rage that exists
between Black men and women
is an open wound slowly
dripping through the years,
causing us to miss each other, dismembered
by our needs and self-righteous vindication
of our egos: Sister/Brother raw with
wounded love, pride and submerged anger,
masks of smiles and hip postures:
games we play to polish our survival
while the wound
bleeds raw, flesh turning rotten
like a half-charred body, dangling
from a lynch-tree, bowing
to the savage wind.

Robert Fleming

FOR ALL UNWED MOTHERS

victims of the demon dance
victims of one night niggers with their hearts
        between their legs.

they moaned to you of their love
        while you were on your back
        with your knees uphigh.

now that their seeds have grown
from the heat of the night ritual
and are screaming for icy souls to love them
        they can't be found

beware sisters, never dance with strangers.

George Barlow

4 1/2 MONTHS: HALFWAY SONG
(Hey, Baby! What you know good?)

Cuddled in the dark,
we place our hands
on the sturdy brown bulb
to feel
the life thumps
of what we've made
with our love.
I tell her
it's a message;
my African son
drumming on the wall.
She tells me
it's my African daughter
dancing to the rhythm
of her own fetal heartbeat.
We agree that
love is a black baby
growing in our hearts.

Horace Coleman

POEM FOR A "DIVORCED" DAUGHTER

if some nosey body asks "well,
is you got a daddy?"
give them the look that
writes "fool" on their face

if that aint enough & they
got to say "where he at?"
tell em "where he be!"

& if they *so* simple they
haven't got it yet
& try to stay in your business

to the degree of "well,
if he love you then how
come he aint here?"
you just sigh

poke your lip out low
ball your hands up
on your hips and let it slip:
"he loves me where he *is*"
    cause I do
    where I am

Eugene B. Redmond

LOVE NECESSITATES

Grandmother's love
Was sometimes her wrath:
    Quick caresses with switch or ironing cord.

My young unhoned hide knew
Volcanic
Voodoo
Vengeance:
Sting-swift payment for unperformed errands and orders;
Rod and wrath for tarrying too long under Black Bridge.

One did not sass Grandma,
Whose love was *stern* and *firm:*
Precise preparation (mercy!)
For the Academy of Hard Knocks.

Haki R. Madhubuti

THE UNION OF TWO

For Ife and Jake

What matters is the renewing and long running kinship
seeking common mission, willing work, memory, melody, song.

marriage is an art,
created by the serious, enjoyed by the mature,
watered with morning and evening promises.

those who grow into love
remain anchored
like egyptian architecture and seasonal flowers.

it is afrikan that woman and man join in smile, tears, future.
it is traditional that men and women share expectations,
        celebrations, struggles.
it is legend that the nations start in the family.
it is afrikan that our circle expands.
it is wise that we believe in tomorrows, children, quality.
it is written that our vision will equal the promise.

so that your nation will live and tell your stories accurately,
you must be endless in your loving touch of each other,
your unification is the message,
continuance the answer.

August 7, 1986

Nikky Finney

UNCLES

mahogany men
with massive hands and broad mustaches
who outlived wars
and married feisty oak-imaged women
be tight with money
tender of heart
and close to me

a gallery of fathers
each of whom planted me
in the well-kept gardens
of their youth
moistened the soil
with vintage tobacco juice
and asked only that i listen
and grow to the rhythms therein

men of mahogany
and oak blossoms
who relaxed late in life
and understood that leaning
was because of trust
not weakness
men who though not supposed to
protected   shielded
their oaks
because as they taught me
love is never what it's supposed to be

Alice Walker

....

DID THIS HAPPEN TO YOUR MOTHER?
DID YOUR SISTER THROW UP A LOT?

I love a man who is not worth
my love.
Did this happen to your mother?
Did your grandmother wake up
for no good reason
in the middle of the night?

I thought love could be controlled.
It cannot.
Only behavior can be controlled.
By biting your tongue purple
rather than speak.
Mauling your lips.
Obliterating his number
too thoroughly
to be able to phone.

Love has made me sick.

Did your sister throw up a lot?
Did your cousin complain
of a painful knot
in her back?
Did your aunt always
seem to have something else
troubling her mind?

I thought love would adapt itself
to my needs.
But needs grow too fast;
they come up like weeds.
Through cracks in the conversation.
Through silences in the dark.
Through everything you thought was concrete.

Such needful love has to be chopped out
or forced to wilt back,
poisoned by disapproval
from its own soil.

This is bad news, for the conservationist.

My hand shakes before this killing.
My stomach sits jumpy in my chest.
My chest is the Grand Canyon
sprawled empty
over the world.

Whoever he is, he is not worth all this.

And I will never
unclench my teeth long enough
to tell him so.

Laini Mataki

NEXT DOOR

so she sd, if u lose me, u lose a good thing.
and he sd, u're right
but there are so many good things
what cld the loss of one good thing be to me.
and she sd yeah, somebody else may groove u, but
nobody will ever luv u like i do.
and he sd, baby that might be true
but the things that these young girls can do, make
a man like me forget about luv   and u.
and she sd, well if u feel like that   f--k u too
and before she cld make it to the door   he was at
his usual place on the floor cryin:
        baby, c'mon baby
and baby wld come
all week, until he messed things up
by stayin out all night.
mornin wld break un-evenly
and she wld say,
        u kno, if u lose me. . . .

Georgia Douglas Johnson

I WANT TO DIE WHILE YOU LOVE ME

I want to die while you love me,
  While yet you hold me fair,
While laughter lies upon my lips
  And lights are in my hair.

I want to die while you love me
  And bear to that still bed
Your kisses turbulent, unspent
  To warm me when I'm dead.

I want to die while you love me
  Oh, who would care to live
Till love has nothing more to ask
  And nothing more to give?

I want to die while you love me
  And never, never see
The glory of this perfect day
  Grow dim or cease to be!

Gloria Wade-Gayles

....

INQUISITION

Do you love her?

Yes.

Do you begin your prayers with her
name?

Yes.

Have you trained the nightingales to
sing
her favorite song, continuously?

Yes.

Have you carved her face on Gibraltar?

Yes.

Have you built a boardwalk over the
oceans
and the seas so that she can walk on
water?

Yes.

Have you traveled through the desert
in search of a velvet cactus just for her?

Yes.

Have you substituted your dreams for
her
nightmares?

Yes.

Do you speak her name in a gentle
whisper
and only with her permission?

Yes.

Do you stroke her back
massage her feet
fluff her pillows
draw her bath
cook her meals
brush her hair
dress her in
      silks and satins
      sables and minks
      pearls diamonds
      rubies ermines
      and glass slippers
      that cannot break?

Yes.

Do you love her?

Yes!
Yes!
Yes!

Is
She
White?

SILENCE.

Ntozake Shange
....
YOU ARE SUCHA FOOL

you are sucha fool/ i haveta love you
you decide to give me a poem/ intent on it/ actually
you pull/ kiss me from 125th to 72nd street/on
the east side/ no less
you are sucha fool/ you gonna give me/ the poet/
the poem
insistin on proletarian images/ we buy okra/
3 lbs for $1/ & a pair of 98¢ shoes
we kiss
we wrestle
you make sure at east 110 street/ we have cognac
no beer all day
you are sucha fool/ you fall over my day like
a wash of azure

you take my tongue outta my mouth/
make me say foolish things
you take my tongue outta my mouth/ lay it on yr skin
like the dew between my legs
on this the first day of silver balloons
& lil girl's braids undone
friendly savage skulls on bikes/ wish me good-day
you speak spanish like a german & ask puerto rican
marketmen on lexington if they are foreigners

oh you are sucha fool/ i cant help but love you
maybe it was something in the air
our memories
our first walk
our first . . .
yes/ alla that

where you poured wine down my throat in rooms
poets i dreamed abt seduced sound & made history/
you make me feel like a cheetah
a gazelle/something fast & beautiful
you make me remember my animal sounds/
so while i am an antelope
ocelot & serpent speaking in tongues
my body loosens for/ you

you decide to give me the poem
you wet yr fingers/ lay it to my lips
that i might write some more abt you/
how you come into me
the way the blues jumps outta b.b. king/ how
david murray assaults a moon & takes her home/
like dyanne harvey invades the wind

oh you/ you are sucha fool/
you want me to write some more abt you
how you come into me like a rollercoaster in a
dip that swings
leaving me shattered/ glistening/ rich/ screeching
& fully clothed

you set me up to fall into yr dreams
like the sub-saharan animal i am/ in all this heat
wanting to be still
to be still with you
in the shadows
all those buildings
all those people/ celebrating/ sunlight & love/ you

you are sucha fool/ you spend all day piling up images
locations/ morsels of daydreams/ to give me a poem

just smile/ i'll get it

TONGUING

tongue lashing
hammer with a frog
giving up the play cuz she got a jones for my scullcap.

Us possibly lovers but things got to change first.
Us possibly lovers but im gon' have to breakdown her mouth
I mean dont you know i called person to person the other day
and heard my own satire twisting outta her end?

You think i be caught up in a lie or something.

Gonna breakdown that mouth for her alright
Weird oxygen hole fulla rank secrets stained by nicotine
And oooh, that tongue
Just a-lashing away lik' she crazy
but way beyond real taste or smell
though
i can smell her tasting
(just gotta know where to catch the smile you dig?)

So i gots to breakdown that mouth for her alright
Bam!/ uh huh.
Except them fine teeth. Keep them. One must have item.
Gon' make me a bad neck hanging mojo
(better for the wear but misunderstood for the overbite.)

She got nice parts elsewhere too.
Not naked but suitable.
Free hands. Maybe she wants to toss me around some.
ok. im game, gregory snake eyes.
Play me. Im game.

Harryette Mullen

....

ROADMAP
for J.R.

She wants a man she can just
unfold when she needs him
then fold him up again
like those 50 cent raincoats
women carry in their purses
in case they get caught in stormy weather.

This one has her thumb out
for a man who's going her way.
She'll hitch with him awhile,
let him take her down the road
for a piece.

But I want to take you where you're going.
I'm unfolding for you
like a roadmap you can never again fold up
exactly the same as before.

Sonia Sanchez

....

HAIKU

i want to make you
roar with laughter as i ride
you into morning.

Sandra Turner Bond
....
TUESDAY NIGHT AFFAIR

i have a lover
who comes through the snow
and i'm waiting
with hot tea and oranges
honey around my cups
there is always cream
in my pantry

i have a lover
who comes through the snow
and i'm waiting
to dance on the ceilings
while stroking his ass
he tries to watch me
suck his most private thoughts
i eat every inch
of his dreams.

E. Ethelbert Miller
....
ANOTHER LOVE AFFAIR/ANOTHER POEM

it was afterwards
when we were in the shower
that she said

"you're gonna write a poem about this"

"about what?" i asked

MY TONGUE PAINTS A PATH

My tongue paints a path of fire
Across her body
My tongue trickles unseen
And indelible tracks
Through the center of her metropolis—
As a flameless torch,
I burn beyond the color
Of heat into infinite fire:
Where her passion
Is onelong sigh of molten air
That my tongue
Banks to a burnsong:
Against the anvil of her geography:
That my tongue *rings*—
Where my tongue plunges plunges
Into the waters of her country—
Into the ravines,
The crops,
Of her forests.

Georgia Douglas Johnson
....

THE HEART OF A WOMAN

The heart of a woman goes forth with the dawn,
As a lone bird, soft winging, so restlessly on,
Afar o'er life's turrets and vales does it roam
In the wake of those echoes the heart calls home.

The heart of a woman falls back with the night,
And enters some alien cage in its plight,
And tries to forget it has dreamed of the stars
While it breaks, breaks, breaks on the sheltering bars.

Gloria Wade-Gayles
....
LOVING AGAIN

Last night
we loved as if the gods
had announced only to us
that the sky would fall
while we slept.

We loved
passionately
selflessly
thinking only of pleasure
giving pleasure,

and I knew I would not grieve
if life should end as you held me.

Daybreak.

The sun slid silently
into our room
kissed our faces
and lay softly
in our love bed.

The sky had not fallen.

The earth had not disappeared.

We were alive
to love again.

James Weldon Johnson
....
SENCE YOU WENT AWAY

Seems lak to me de stars don't shine so bright,
Seems lak to me de sun done loss his light,
Seems lak to me der's nothin' goin' right,
   Sence you went away.

Seems lak to me de sky ain't half so blue,
Seems lak to me dat ev'ything wants you,
Seems lak to me I don't know what to do,
   Sence you went away.

Seems lak to me dat ev'ything is wrong,
Seems lak to me de day's jes twice es long,
Seems lak to me de bird's forgot his song,
   Sence you went away.

Seems lak to me I jes can't he'p but sigh,
Seems lak to me ma th'oat keeps gittin' dry,
Seems lak to me a tear stays in ma eye,
   Sence you went away.

Pearl Cleage

CONFESSION

If I lie naked
with my gloves
folded
on the table,
my lips parted,
do not think it is
true
that I love you.
I still wear my
hat.

Melvin Dixon

PLACE, PLACES

First night you were gone
I heard fingers scratching,
clawing from the closet walls.
Some mouse maybe, some thing
was caught between stud beams
and plaster. All next day
it tried to dig through, to nest
in your sheets and blankets
tiny paws, teeth, and nose
in a desperate bid for air.

Then all was quiet.
I looked for the gnawed exit,
footprints, any other signs
of quick release, but nothing found.

Slowly filling from room to room
was the smell of dead flesh and fur.
I opened every window against
the silence and the odorous fusion
of bones into the architecture.

I cleaned the closet anyway,
emptied trash, washed dishes
I had dirtied all alone, remade
the bed with each corner in tight.
Here in full view is a place for me
again. You come home hungry, tired.
And I return from a different journey,
my hands stirring the air, air.

Etheridge Knight
....
AS YOU LEAVE ME

Shiny record albums scattered over
the livingroom floor, reflecting light
from the lamp, sharp reflections that hurt
my eyes as I watch you, squatting among the platters,
the beer foam making mustaches on your lips.

And, too,
the shadows on your cheeks from your long lashes
fascinate me—almost as much as the dimples:
in your cheeks, your arms and your legs:
dimples . . . dimples . . . dimples . . .

You
hum along with Mathis—how you love Mathis!
with his burnished hair and quicksilver voice that dances
among the stars and whirls through canyons
like windblown snow. sometimes I think that Mathis
could take you from me if you could be complete
without me. I glance at my watch. it is now time.

You rise,
silently, and to the bedroom and the paint:
on the lips red, on the eyes black,
and I lean in the doorway and smoke, and see you
grow old before my eyes, and smoke. why do you
chatter while you dress, and smile when you grab
your large leather purse? don't you know that when you
leave me I walk to the window and watch you? and light
a reefer as I watch you? and I die as I watch you
disappear in the dark streets
to whistle and to smile at the johns.

DEALING SCRAPS

I must have back this breath
you take away
dryly
like wine.

Your love
is formidable, like night
and certain prodding
to sobs.

When you leave
it is with nothing left;
weird shadows
haunt the light
and my gaunt reflection
in glass.

I have lingered
at my neighbor's house
to steal from time
and her sorrows

I seek out strangers.

In my own house
I am stranger
to the thick presence
of your absence.

For these hours
I invent
importances. These thoughts
have pulled all threads.
My mind lies limp.

Your lust carried me
to this trickery
when you racked the crannies of
my woman's heart.
I do not think
I can no longer
make magic.

I have exhausted
patience. Every thing
has drained away

except this desperate love.
except this desperate love.

Norman Jordan

....

WHEN A WOMAN GETS BLUE

No man knows
How empty a woman feels
When she gets blue.
When her man is gone
And troubles call,
No man knows.
When a woman's been trying
When a woman's been suffering,
No man knows.
When a woman is alone,
When a woman feels un-needed

No man knows.
When all the world seems cold
And a woman cries
No man knows.
When a woman's heart aches
And her lips are silent
No man knows
No man knows
The lonely hurt
When a woman gets blue.

Patricia Jones

....

SONG

i have so little sorrow
all them blues that followed me
for so long have gone on off
somewhere else to drive another
woman almost mad
the sun shines at my back door
birds sing outside my window
although this is the city
and the tears that marked my
face have dyed my skin a deeper
hue
a color full of blood and learning
and now i know that
grief can't stay in a healthy house
oh
i have so little sorrow
them blues them bad bad blues
have gone on off somewhere else
to drive another woman
almost mad.

IT IS NOT JUST

it is not just
the rain   /no   there is too much
magic in this day
flowers unfold their throats
to the sky & the air is splattered
with the scent of green & not just rain
no/ them hussy clouds sashayed over
spilling their bosoms in the face of the sun
& he split   leaving a hole
where a sunset could be
and the quiet storm just a melody in smokey's head
or a mythical place on a radio dial that wish
it was as real as the dance of liquid
time steps glidin across my roof,
testifyin to record levels of hoodoo going down
on a day when the sun got hisself seduced
out the sky
obatala woke me before dawn
cut away sleep from my eye
leaving a flood of stars in my mouth
& my mind sharp as a blade,
senses humming like a river of lights,
limbs divining trembling tributaries to the past
& I can see forever between raindrops
& there is mystery
even in the absence of the moon
whitefolks lookin at me strange & only a limited number
of colored will admit their complicity
with the magic present, here, in this day
but i am the one wet with words
& even the jars i put around my bed to catch
all the poems fallin through the cracks
in my roof, can't contain the colors,
nascent & shimmering, like new music,
fallin & spinnin & getting caught up
in my hair & on my skin & everywhere i look
it is there   out here
floatin   too much magic
out here
in this day

A POEM LOOKING FOR A READER

(to be read with a love consciousness)

black is not
all inclusive,
there are other colors.
color her warm and womanly,
color her feeling and life,
color her a gibran poem & 4 women of simone.
children will give her color
paint her the color of her
man.

most of all color her
love
a remembrance of life
a truereflection
that we
will
move   u will move with
i want
u
a fifty minute call to blackwomanworld:
                  hi baby,
                    how u doin?
need u.
listening to
young-holt's, *please sunshine, please.*

....

to give   i'll give
most personal.
what about the other
scenes: children playing in vacant lots,
              or like the first time u knowingly kissed a girl,
              was it joy or just beautifully beautiful.

i
remember at 13
reading chester himes'
cast the first stone and
the eyes of momma when she caught me: read on, son.

how will u come:
              like a soulful strut in a two-piece beige o-rig'i-nal,
              or afro-down with a beat in yr/walk?
how will love come:
              painless and deep like a razor cut
              or like some cheap 75 ¢ movie;
              i think not.

will she be the woman
other men will want or
will her beauty be
accented with my name on it?

she will come as she would
want her man to come.
she'll come,
she'll come.
i
never wrote a love letter
but
that doesn't mean
i
don't love.

Vega

BROTHERS LOVING BROTHERS

Respect yourself, my brother,
for we are so many wondrous things.

Like a black rose,
you are a rarity to be found.
Our leaves intertwine as I reach out to you
after the release of a gentle rain.

You precious gem,
black pearl that warms the heart,
symbol of ageless wisdom,
I derive strength
from the touch of your hand.

Our lives blend together
like rays of light;
we are men of color,
adorned in shades of tan, red,
beige, black, and brown.

Brothers born from the same earth womb.
Brothers reaching for the same star.

Love me as your equal.
Love me, brother to brother.

Haki R. Madhubuti

··········

MY BROTHERS

my brothers i will not tell you
who to love or not love
i will only say to you
that
Black women have not been
loved enough.

i will say to you
that
we are at war & that
Black men in america are
being removed from the
earth
like loose sand in a wind storm
and that the women Black are
three to each of us.

no
my brothers i will not tell you
who to love or not love
but
i will make you aware of our
self hating and hurting ways.
make you aware of whose bellies
you dropped from.
i will glue your ears to those images
you reflect which are not being
loved.

Ntozake Shange
....

WHERE THE MISSISSIPPI MEETS THE AMAZON
(for david murray)

you fill me up so much
when you touch me
i cant stay here
i haveta go to my space

people talk to me
try to sell me cocaine
play me a tune
somebody wanted to give me a massage
but i waz thinkin abt you
so i waz in my space

i'm so into it
i cant even take you

tho i ran there with you
tho you appear to me by the riverbed

i cant take you
it's my space
a land lovin you gives me

shall i tell you how my country looks
my soil & rains
there's a point where the amazon meets the mississippi
a bodega squats on the eiffel tower
toward mont saint michel

i'm so into it
i cant even take you
it's my space
a land lovin you gives me

there's a bistro there near the pacific
& the pyramid of the moon is under my bed
i can see the ferry from trois islets to rio
from my window/ yr eyes caress my shoulders

....

my space is a realm of monuments & water
language & the ambiance of senegalese cafes

i cant take you tho
you send me packin/ for anywhere/ i've never known
where we never not exist
in my country we are/ always
you know how you kiss me
just like that

where the nile flows into the ganges
how the arc de triomphe is next to penn station
where stevie wonder sleeps in a d$^\#$ whole note
& albert ayler is not in the east river

my space
where i sip chablis from yr mouth
& grow roses in my womb

where the mississippi meets the amazon
neruda still tangoes in santiago at dawn
where i live

jean-jacques dessalines is continually re-elected
the moon sometimes scarlet

i cant take you
but i'll tell you
all i can remember
when you touch me

June Jordan

GRAND ARMY PLAZA
for Ethelbert

Why would anybody build a monument to civil war?

The tall man and myself tonight
we will not sleep together
we may not
either one of us
sleep
in any case
the differential between friend and lover
is a problem
definitions curse
as *nowadays we're friends*
or
we were lovers once
while
overarching the fastidious the starlit
dust
that softens space between us
is the history that bleeds
through shirt and blouse
alike

the stain of skin on stone

But on this hard ground curved by memories
of union and disunion and of brothers dead
by the familiar hand

how do we face to face a man
a woman
interpenetrated
free
and reaching still toward the kiss that will
not suffocate?

We are not survivors of a civil war

We survive our love
because we go on

loving

Primus St. John

SUNDAY

Today,
The sea has its own religion,
It is as blue
As an acori bead
I rubbed in my hand.

I think
Of swimming out
   for miles
      and miles
         in prayer.

I think
Of never struggling back
In doubt.

As though
In a world like this
Love starts over and over again.

Jayne Cortez

PRAY FOR THE LOVERS

Pray for the lovers
for those who are suspicious
for those who are jealous
for those who are revengeful
Pray for the lovers
for those who are unsatisfied for
those who are frightened for
those who are disappointed
pray for those who are lonely lazy & limited
Pray for the lovers
for those unwilling to reveal & unable to revolt
for those who are helpless
those who are hostile
for those whose flesh goes dead upon touching
the frigid
the passive
the latent

the soft
have mercy on the lovers in heat
pray for those with pain in their bodies
pain in their minds
for sorrow
for fear &
the spell of madness after love says goodby
Pray for the lovers in the name of love
in the name of god &
the mirror of death
love in the name of some rollin hips
those churning lips & the blood
that drips incest to
incest
all power to the lovers in the name of love
all power to the lovers in the name of love
all power to the lovers in the name of love

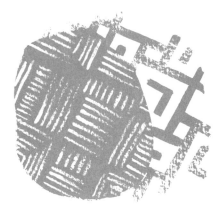

FAMILY GATHERINGS

A. B. Spellman

WHEN BLACK PEOPLE ARE

when black people are
with each other
we sometimes fear ourselves
whisper over our shoulders
about unmentionable acts
& sometimes we fight & lie.
these are somethings we sometimes do.

& when alone i sometimes walk
from wall to wall fighting visions
of white men fighting me
& black men fighting white men
& fighting me & i lose my
self between walls &
ricocheting shots & can't say
for certain who i have killed
or been killed by.

it is the fear of winter passing
& summer coming & the killing
i have called for coming
to my door saying
hit it a.b., you're in it too.

& the white army moves like thieves
in the night mass producing beautiful
black corpses & then stealing them away
while my frequent death watches me
from orangeburg on cronkite &
i'm oiling my gun & cooking my food
& saying "when the time comes"
to myself, over & over, hopefully.

but i remember driving from atlanta
to the city with stone & featherstone
& cleve & on the way feather talked
about ambushing a pair of klansmen
& cleve told how they hunted
chaney's body in the white night
of the haunted house in the mississippi
swamp while a runaway survivor
from orangeburg slept between wars
on the back seat.

times like this
are times when black people
are with each other & the strength flows
back & forth between us like
borrowed breath.

Amiri Baraka

··········

KA 'BA

A closed window looks down
on a dirty courtyard, and black people
call across or scream across or walk across
defying physics in the stream of their will

Our world is full of sound
Our world is more lovely than anyone's
tho we suffer, and kill each other
and sometimes fail to walk the air

We are beautiful people
with african imaginations
full of masks and dances and swelling chants
with african eyes, and noses, and arms,

though we sprawl in gray chains in a place
full of winters, when what we want is sun.

We have been captured,
brothers. And we labor
to make our getaway, into
the ancient image, into a new

correspondence with ourselves
and our black family. We need magic
now we need the spells, to raise up
return, destroy, and create. What will be

the sacred words?

Gerald Barrax

··········

STRANGERS LIKE US:
PITTSBURGH, RALEIGH, 1945–1985

The sounds our parents heard echoing over
housetops while listening to evening radios
were the uninterrupted cries running and cycling
we sent through the streets and yards, where spring summer
fall we were entrusted to the night, boys and
girls together, to send us home for bath and
bed after the dark had drifted down and eased
contests between pitcher and batter, hider and seeker.

Our own children live imprisoned in light.
They are cycloned into our yards and hearts,
whose gates flutter shut on unfamiliar smiles.
At the rumor of a moon, we call them in
before the monsters who hunt, who hurt, who haunt
us, rise up from our own dim streets.

Jay Wright

....

WEDNESDAY NIGHT PRAYER MEETING

On Wednesday night,
the church still opens at seven,
and the boys and girls have to come in
from their flirting games of tag,
with the prayers they've memorized,
the hymns they have to start.
Some will even go down front,
with funky bibles,
to read verses from Luke,
where Jesus triumphs, or Revelations,
where we all come to no good end.
Outside, the pagan kids
scramble in the darkness,
kissing each other with a sly humility,
or urinating boldly against the trees.
The older people linger
in the freshly lit night,
not in a hurry to enter,
having been in the battle of voices
far too long, knowing that the night
will stretch and end only
when some new voice rises
in ecstasy, or deceit, only
when some arrogant youth
comes cringing down front,
screaming about sin, begging
the indifferent faced women
for a hand, for a touch,
for a kiss, for help,
for forgiveness, for being young
and untouched by the grace
of pain, innocent of the insoluble
mysteries of being black
and sinned against, black
and sinning in the compliant cities.
What do the young know
about some corpulent theologian,
sitting under his lamp,
his clammy face wet,

his stomach trying to give up
the taste of a moderate wine,
kissing God away with a labored
toss of his pen?
How would these small black singers
know which Jesus is riding
there over the pulpit,
in the folds of the banner
left over from Sunday,
where the winners were the ones
who came, who dropped their nickels
into the felted platters with a flourish?
And how can they be expected
to remember the cadences
that will come again,
the same heart-rending release
of the same pain, as the clock turns
toward the certainty
of melancholic afternoons,
roast and left-over prayers,
the dampened hours that last through the night?
But Christ will come,
feeling injured, having gone
where beds were busy without him,
having seen pimps cane their number running boys,
the televisions flicker over heaped up bodies,
having heard some disheveled man
shout down an empty street, where women
slither in plastic boots, toward light,
their eyes dilated and empty;
will come like a tired workman
and sit on a creaky bench,
in hope, in fear, wanting to be pleased again,
so anxious that his hands move,
his head tilts for any lost accent.
He seems to be home,
where he's always been.
His intense smile is fixed
to the rhythm of hands,

to the unhurried intensity
of this improvised singing.
He seems not to know
the danger of being here,
among these lonely singers,
in the middle of a war
of spirits who will not wait for him,
who cannot take his intense glare
to heart anymore, who cannot justify
the Wednesday nights given up
in these stuffy, tilted rooms,
while the work piles up for Thursday,
and the dogs mope around empty garbage pails,
and the swingers swing into the night
with a different ecstasy.
Caught in this unlovely music,
he spills to the floor.
The sisters circle him,
and their hands leap from bone to bone,
as if their touch would change him,
would make him see
the crooked lights like stars.
The bible-reading boy tags him with verses,
and he writhes like a boy
giving up stolen kisses,
the free play of his hand on his own body,
the unholy clarity of his worldly speech.
He writhes as if he would be black,

on Wednesday, under the uncompromising
need of old black men and women,
who know that pain is what
you carry in the mind,
in the solemn memory of small triumphs,
that you get, here,
as the master of your pain.
He stands up to sing,
but a young girl,
getting up from the mourner's bench,
tosses her head in a wail.
The women rise,
the men collect the banners
and the boys drop their eyes,
listening to the unearthly wind
whisper to the peeping-tom trees.
This is the end of the night,
and he has not come there yet,
has not made it into the stillness
of himself, or the flagrant uncertainty
of all these other singers.
They have taken his strangeness,
and given it back, the way a lover
will return the rings and letters
of a lover that hurts him.
They have closed their night
with what certainty they could,
unwilling to change their freedom for a god.

FAMILY GATHERINGS

Robert Hayden
....

THOSE WINTER SUNDAYS

Sundays too my father got up early
and put his clothes on in the blueblack cold,
then with cracked hands that ached
from labor in the weekday weather made
banked fires blaze. No one ever thanked him.

I'd wake and hear the cold splintering, breaking.
When the rooms were warm, he'd call,
and slowly I would rise and dress,
fearing the chronic angers of that house,

Speaking indifferently to him,
who had driven out the cold
and polished my good shoes as well.
What did I know, what did I know
of love's austere and lonely offices?

Michael S. Weaver
....

THE PICNIC, AN HOMAGE TO CIVIL RIGHTS

We spread torn quilts and blankets,
mashing the grass under us until it was hard,
piled the baskets of steamed crabs
by the trees in columns that hid the trunk,
put our water coolers of soda pop
on the edges to mark the encampment,
like gypsies settling in for revelry
in a forest in Rumania or pioneers
blazing through the land of the Sioux,
the Apache, and the Arapaho, looking guardedly
over our perimeters for poachers
or the curious noses of fat women
ambling past on the backs of their shoes.
The sun crashed through the trees,
tumbling down and splattering in shadows

on the baseball diamond like mashed bananas.
We hunted for wild animals in the clumps
of forests, fried hot dogs until the odor
turned solid in our nostrils like wood.
We were in the park.

One uncle talked incessantly, because he knew
the universe; another was the griot
who stomped his foot in syncopation
to call the details from the base of his mind;
another was a cynic who doubted everything,
toasting everyone around with gin.
The patriarchal council mumbled on,
while the women took the evening to tune
their hearts to the slow air and buzzing flies,
to hold their hands out so angels could stand
in their palms and give dispensation,
as we played a rough game of softball
in the diamond with borrowed gloves,
singing Chuck Berry and Chubby Checker,
diving in long lines into the public pool,
throwing empty peanut shells to the lion,
buying cotton candy in the aviary
of the old mansion, laughing at monkeys,
running open-mouthed and full in the heat
until our smell was pungent and natural,
while the sun made our fathers and uncles
fall down in naps on their wives' laps, and
we frolicked like wealthy children on an English estate,
as reluctant laws and bloodied heads
tacked God's theses on wooden doors,
guaranteed the canopy of the firmament above us.

Michael S. Harper

....

BREADED MEAT, BREADED HANDS

The heat of the oven
glazed on the windowed
doors, the percolated lines
of water drizzle down;
she cooks over the heated
fires in a blaze of meat.

The shelled pan-baked peanuts
ground to a paste
pass over the chicken
ripped off by tornadoes.

Raisins of my son's eyes
garnish the pork loin,
kidneys and beef heart.

In the corner the rock salt
and the crushed snow
churn the coconut
ice cream, vanilla
beans and two half pints
of cream atop the thundering
washing machine.

Boards thick with sweet potatoes,
the piecrust cooled in the icebox,
dough souring on the stove top,
the hands of our children
damp with flour and butter
of their burning skins,
and the marks of cooking,
churnings of the heated kitchen.

Yogurt to cover the cucumbers,
sautéed onions, the curd of some
cabbaged blood wine, bottled
vinegar which tastes like olive oil.

At the hearth of this house,
my woman, cutting the bits of guile,
the herbs of warmth she has butchered
into the pots,
the pans of grease
that feed this room, and our children,
condensed in the opaque room —
the hearth of this house
is this woman, the strength of the bread
in her hands, the meat in her marrow
and of her blood.

Lenard D. Moore

....

WINTER 1967

One hard cold after another came
and brutally took our house over like a terrorist.
I remember my mother walking
through the house like a prison guard.
She gathered us, my brothers, sisters and me,
and led us to the bedroom.
Holding the youngest child's hand,
she said, "All of you get in this bed
and pile the blankets on top of you."

What my mother told us
I do not have to tell my daughter,
because we have central heat,
and I am home to keep it running.
My father was in Vietnam that winter,
low-crawling in the fiery jungles,
and zigzagging through rice paddies.
My mother was too short to lift
and pour five gallons of oil
into the drum.
I was so cold inside my bones
I would have strained to pour the oil.

I cannot get over my father
having to abandon us.
I knew he would never leave us
if he didn't have to.
Yet pain sizzled in me.
Lying on my back, a boy of nine,
I'd stare at my father's picture on the wall,
a stranger staring at me,
and see him in my sleep,
lifting huge cans of oil like a crane.

Marilyn Nelson Waniek

BALI HAI CALLS MAMA

As I was putting away the groceries
I'd spent the morning buying
for the week's meals I'd planned
around things the baby could eat,
things my husband would eat,
and things I should eat
because they aren't too fattening,
late on a Saturday afternoon
after flinging my coat on a chair
and wiping the baby's nose
while asking my husband
what he'd fed it for lunch
and whether
the medicine I'd brought for him
had made his cough improve,
wiping the baby's nose again,
checking its diaper,
stepping over the baby
who was reeling to and from
the bottom kitchen drawer
with pots, pans, and plastic cups,
occasionally clutching the hem of my skirt
and whining to be held,
I was half listening for the phone
which never rings for me
to ring for me
and someone's voice to say that
I could forget about handing back
my students' exams which I'd had for a week,
that I was right about *The Waste Land,*
that I'd been given a raise,
all the time wondering
how my sister was doing,
whatever happened to my old lover(s),
and why my husband wanted
a certain brand of toilet paper;
and I wished I hadn't, but I'd bought
another fashion magazine that promised

to make me beautiful by Christmas,
and there wasn't room for the creamed corn
and every time I opened the refrigerator door
the baby rushed to grab whatever was on the bottom shelf
which meant I constantly had to wrestle
jars of its mushy food out of its sticky hands
and I stepped on the baby's hand and the baby was screaming
and I dropped the bag of cake flour I'd bought to make cookies with
and my husband rushed in to find out what was wrong because the baby
was drowning out the sound of the touchdown although I had scooped
it up and was holding it in my arms so its crying was inside
my head like an echo in a barrel and I was running cold water
on its hand while somewhere in the back of my mind wondering what
to say about *The Waste Land* and whether I could get away with putting
broccoli in a meatloaf when

suddenly through the window
came the wild cry of geese.

Nancy Travis
....

AT MY FATHER'S HOUSE

In the kitchen as the toast browns
I put on my 3rd grade cateye glasses
pearly blue with rhinestone tips
I found with the baby books.
Music's echoing into the room
from the radio my brother hooked up
in the bathroom upstairs.
I prance to the refrigerator,
doing tina turner
making my dress into a mini skirt
to get some juice.
then my father comes in
& shakes his head
saying
four years' money for college
gone straight
down the drain

Nikki Giovanni

KNOXVILLE, TENNESSEE

I always like summer
best
you can eat fresh corn
from daddy's garden
and okra
and greens
and cabbage
and lots of
barbecue
and buttermilk
and homemade ice-cream
at the church picnic
and listen to
gospel music
outside
at the church
homecoming
and go to the mountains with
your grandmother
and go barefooted
and be warm
all the time
not only when you go to bed
and sleep

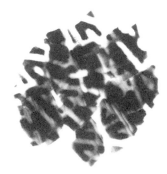

Rita Dove

FIFTH GRADE AUTOBIOGRAPHY

I was four in this photograph fishing
with my grandparents at a lake in Michigan.
My brother squats in poison ivy.
His Davy Crockett cap
sits squared on his head so the raccoon tail
flounces down the back of his sailor suit.

My grandfather sits to the far right
in a folding chair,
and I know his left hand is on
the tobacco in his pants pocket
because I used to wrap it for him
every Christmas. Grandmother's hips
bulge from the brush, she's leaning
into the ice chest, sun through the trees
printing her dress with soft
luminous paws.

I am staring jealously at my brother;
the day before he rode his first horse, alone.
I was strapped in a basket
behind my grandfather.
He smelled of lemons. He's died —

but I remember his hands.

Marilyn Nelson Waniek

....

SLEEPLESS NIGHTS

We used to tell each other erotic stories
at slumber parties when I was about ten:
We'd meet and kiss dark, handsome boys,
and then sink into sixty-year dreams
from which we'd wake up for church weddings
and to name our butterscotch babies.
From there we always jumped ahead
to the pooping-out party, and died laughing
into our silencing pillows at the way
we'd overdose on laxatives, and be dead.

We never dreamed of the face-making
self-reconstruction from scratch
we'd be engaged in for most of our lives,
of at thirty-four an ordinary day
on which an aspiration is adjusted down
another notch like a dress let out twice
at the waist, then finally given away,
of the rambling Victorian responsibilities we'd own,
full of furniture that doesn't match
and appliances that always need kicking.

We carefully flushed away the traces
of the filched cigarettes we'd tried
before our two o'clock forays in the dark,
then we raced back on tiptoe to devour
unsweetened chocolate, olives, laundry starch,
and in our floppy pajamas, giggled for hours.

When we made out each others' drawn faces
by the first pale murmurs of light
we were stupefied
to see how old we could grow overnight.

childhood remembrances are always a drag
if you're Black
you always remember things like living in Woodlawn
with no inside toilet
and if you become famous or something
they never talk about how happy you were to have your mother
all to yourself and
how good the water felt when you got your bath from one of those
big tubs that folk in chicago barbecue in
and somehow when you talk about home
it never gets across how much you
understood their feelings
as the whole family attended meetings about Hollydale
and even though you remember
your biographers never understand
your father's pain as he sells his stock
and another dream goes
and though you're poor it isn't poverty that
concerns you
and though they fought a lot
it isn't your father's drinking that makes any difference
but only that everybody is together and you
and your sister have happy birthdays and very good christmasses
and I really hope no white person ever has cause to write about me
because they never understand Black love is Black wealth and they'll
probably talk about my hard childhood and never understand that
all the while I was quite happy

Reuben Jackson

SUNDAY BRUNCH

and where
do your parents
summer?
she asked
him.

the front porch,
he replied.

Brian G. Gilmore

BOW TO ALLAH

in america
people
treat
christmas
like
the hajj

only
mecca
is a
mall.

Nikki Giovanni
....
THE WOMEN GATHER
(for Joe Strickland)

the women gather
because it is not unusual
to seek comfort in our hours of stress
    a man must be buried

it is not unusual
that the old bury the young
    though it is an abomination

it is not strange
that the unwise and the ungentle
carry the banner of humaneness
    though it is a castration of the spirit

it no longer shatters the intellect
that those who make war
call themselves diplomats

we are no longer surprised
that the unfaithful pray loudest
every sunday in every church
and sometimes in rooms facing east
    though it is a sin and a shame

    so how do we judge a man

most of us love from our need to love not
because we find someone deserving

most of us forgive because we have trespassed not
because we are magnanimous

most of us comfort because we need comforting
our ancient rituals demand that we give
what we hope to receive

    and how do we judge a man

we learn to greet when meeting
to cry when parting
and to soften our words at times of stress

the women gather
with cloth and ointment
their busy hands bowing to laws that decree
willows shall stand swaying but unbroken
against even the determined wind of death

we judge a man by his dreams
not alone his deeds
we judge a man by his intent
not alone his shortcomings
we judge a man because it is not unusual
to know him through those who love him

the women gather strangers
to each other because
they have loved a man

it is not unusual to sift
through ashes
and find an unburnt picture

Carolyn Rodgers
....
GROUP THERAPY

the bathroom
is a meeting place
for all of my me's
cigarettes, magazine, pencils, paper,
we all sit there
and stare at each other
and wonder if
anything will come out right.

SATURDAY AFTERNOON, WHEN CHORES ARE DONE

I've cleaned house
and the kitchen smells like pine.
I can hear the kids yelling
through the back screen door.
While they play tug-of-war
with an old jumprope
and while these blackeyed peas
boil on the stove,
I'm gonna sit here at the table
and plait my hair.

I oil my hair and brush it soft.
Then, with the brush in my lap,
I gather the hair in my hands,
pull the strands smooth and tight,
and weave three sections into a fat shiny braid
that hangs straight down my back.

I remember mama teaching me to plait my hair
one Saturday afternoon when chores were done.
My fingers were stubby and short.
I could barely hold three strands at once,
and my braids would fray apart
no sooner than I'd finished them.
Mama said, "Just takes practice, is all."
Now my hands work swiftly, doing easy
what was once so hard to do.

Between time on the job,
keeping house, and raising two girls by myself,
there's never much time like this,
for thinking and being alone.
Time to gather life together
before it unravels like an old jumprope
and comes apart at the ends.

Suddenly I notice the silence.
The noisy tug-of-war has stopped.
I get up to check out back,
see what my girls are up to now.
I look out over the kitchen sink,
where the sweet potato plant
spreads green in the window.
They sit quietly on the back porch steps,
Melinda plaiting Carla's hair
into a crooked braid.

Older daughter,
you are learning what I am learning:
to gather the strands together
with strong fingers,
to keep what we do
from coming apart at the ends.

WHEN MALINDY SINGS

G'way an' quit dat noise, Miss Lucy —
    Put dat music book away;
What's de use to keep on tryin'?
    Ef you practise twell you're gray,
You cain't sta't no notes a-flyin'
    Lak de ones dat rants and rings
From the kitchen to de big woods
    When Malindy sings.

You ain't got de nachel o'gans
    Fu' to make de soun' come right,
You ain't got de tu'ns an' twistin's
    Fu' to make it sweet an' light.
Tell you one thing now, Miss Lucy,
    An' I'm tellin' you fu' true,
When hit comes to raal right singin',
    Tain't no easy thing to do.

Easy 'nough fu' folks to hollah,
    Lookin' at de lines an' dots,
When dey ain't no one kin sence it,
    An' de chune comes in, in spots;
But fu' real melojous music,
    Dat jes' strikes yo' hea't and clings,
Jes' you stan' an listen wif me
    When Malindy sings.

Ain't you nevah hyeahd Malindy?
    Blessed soul, tek up de cross!
Look hyeah, ain't you jokin', honey?
    Well, you don't know whut you los'.
Y'ought to hyeah dat gal a-wa'blin',
    Robins, la'ks, an' all dem things,
Heish dey moufs an' hides dey faces
    When Malindy sings.

Fiddlin' man jes' stop his fiddlin',
    Lay his fiddle on de she'f;
Mockin'-bird quit tryin' to whistle,
    'Cause he jes' so shamed hisse'f.

Folks a-playin' on de banjo
    Draps dey fingahs on de strings —
Bless yo' soul — fu'gits to move 'em,
    When Malindy sings.

She jes' spreads huh mouf and hollahs,
    "Come to Jesus," twell you hyeah
Sinnahs' tremblin' steps and voices,
    Timid-lak a-drawin' neah;
Den she tu'ns to "Rock of Ages,"
    Simply to de cross she clings,
An' you fin' yo' teahs a-drappin'
    When Malindy sings.

Who dat says dat humble praises
    Wif de Master nevah counts?
Heish yo' mouf, I hyeah dat music,
    Ez hit rises up an' mounts —
Floatin' by de hills an' valleys,
    Way above dis buryin' sod,
Ez hit makes its way in glory
    To de very gates of God!

Oh, hit's sweetah dan de music
    Of an edicated band;
An' hit's dearah dan de battle's
    Song o' triumph in de lan'.
It seems holier than evenin'
    When de solemn chu'ch bell rings,
Ez I sit an' ca'mly listen
    While Malindy sings.

Towsah, stop dat ba'kin', hyeah me!
    Mandy, mek dat chile keep still;
Don't you hyeah de echoes callin'
    From de valley to de hill?
Let me listen, I can hyeah it,
    Th'oo de bresh of angel's wings,
Sof' an' sweet, "Swing Low, Sweet Chariot,"
    Ez Malindy sings.

Safiya Henderson-Holmes
·········

GOODHOUSEKEEPING #17
(kitchen fable)

it was early in the morning
before sun or her children rose
and she was at the kitchen sink squeezing
pink liquid soap over the previous nights dishes
and she had pink curlers in her hair
and a pink, frayed, terrycloth robe drooped over her
shoulders
and a worn bra and an over bleached
pair of panties peeked
from under the pink robe every now and then

and she ran hot water over the dishes and over her hands
and she looked into a bubble and popped it with her spit
and then it happened
right there in the early morning, in her kitchen sink,
before her own never enough sleep eyes
rose mr. clean

with his gold earring in his left ear
and his big hands on his hips and his hips,
hands, face, legs all golden yellowish
with a pale green glow all around
and she put her soapy hands over her wide opened
mouth. then to her stiffened in disbelief neck
and mr. clean with his gold earring in his left ear,
and his hands on his hips,
and his hips all golden and muscular, winked at her
and sparks of light flew from his eyelid

and she covered her breast and mr. clean smiled and
sparks of light shot from his snow white teeth
and she picked up a nearby knife
and mr. clean said — i can make your work disappear —
and she held her robe closed with one hand
and raised the knife higher with the other
and mr. clean pulled on his gold earring
and the knife and every dirty dish disappeared

and she reached for her curlers
as though expecting them to go too
and mr. clean shook his gleaming, hairless head at the
stove and every pot and pan disappeared
and the stove sparkled
she swayed into a faint, her head bowed, her knees bent,
her eyes rolled, her hands flew way above her head
and mr. clean saw her go down and scooped her up
and held her close
& his ammonia and pine like sudsy smell revived her
and he said,
— i could make your life more enjoyable —

and he pulled on his gold earring in his left ear
and her curlers left, her robe went, and the worn bra
and over bleached panties were zapped away
and she was butt naked in the arms of mr. clean
she didn't know what to do, she was speechless
swore her eyes had gone totally bad

and mr. clean said — i could make it real good for you —
and he smiled and sparks of light covered her thighs
and in all her years of standing at her kitchen sink,
her thighs had never been touched by anything,
let alone light and she looked at her thighs all aglow,
she looked at her sink and stove all aglow
and she looked at a roach who had been watching
the whole damn thing
and she felt something warm
and itchy rise from her stomach to the tip of her head

and in all her years of being in the kitchen, she had never
been as warm before, and she had never been
held as close before
and she braved a look into mr. clean's golden eyes,
braved a touch of his gold earring
and somehow, from somewhere
words swelled in her neck and she said,
as she held on to the gold earring

— could you make me shine mister, could you really,
really, make me shine forever more —

Nancy Travis

CHURCH LADIES

they wear big felt hats
and are flatsweet smelling
like the heavy thick glossy
pages of museum picture books,
they play bingo on wednesdays
and make biscuits once loved
by their dead or ex-husbands.
when you see one downtown
she will urge you to come
to the church dinner Sunday
and say
please dear
do bring your unsaved friends.

Cornelius Eady
....
MY MOTHER IS A GOD FEARING WOMAN

everytime a thunderstorm comes
my mother turns off the electricity in our house.
she is a god fearing woman.
CLICK! off goes the t.v.
CLICK! off goes the living room light.
CLICK! off goes the kitchen light.
CLICK! off goes the radio.
CLICK! the house falls into darkness.
my mother is a god fearing woman.

we sit all together in one room and listen to
the rain fall around us till we fall off to sleep.

my mother is a god-fearing woman.

Harryette Mullen
....
MOMMA SAYINGS

Momma had words for us:
We were "crumb crushers,"
"eating machines,"
"bottomless pits."
Still, she made us charter members
of the bonepickers' club,
saying, "Just don't let your eyes
get bigger than your stomach."
Saying, "Take all you want,
but eat all you take."
Saying, "I'm not made of money, you know,
and the man at the Safeway
don't give away groceries for free."

She trained us not to leave lights on
"all over the house,"
because "electricity costs money
so please turn the lights off when you leave a room
and take the white man's hand out of my pocket."

When we were small
she called our feet "ant mashers,"
but each time we'd outgrow our shoes,
our feet became "platforms."
She told us we must be growing big feet
to support some big heavyset women
(like our grandma Tiddly).

When she had to buy us new underwear
to replace the old ones full of holes,
she'd swear we were growing razor blades in our behinds,
"you tear these draws up so fast."

Momma had words for us, all right:
she called us "the wrecking crew."
She said our untidy bedroom
looked like "a cyclone struck it."

Our dirty fingernails she called "victory gardens."
And when we'd come in from playing outside
she'd tell us, "You girls smell like iron rust."
She'd say, "Go take a bath
and get some of that funk off of you."
But when the water ran too long in the tub
she'd yell, "That's enough water to wash an elephant."
And after the bath she'd say,
"Be sure and grease those ashy legs."
She'd lemon-creme our elbows
and pull the hot comb
through "these tough kinks on your heads."

Momma had lots of words for us,
her never-quite-perfect daughters,
the two brown pennies
she wanted to polish
so we'd shine like dimes.

BARBERSHOP RITUAL

Baby brother can't wait.
For him, the rite of passage
begins early — before obligatory heists
of candy & comic books from neighborhood
stores, before street battles to claim
turf, before he might gain
the title "Man of the House"
before his time.

Each week, he steps up to the chair,
the closest semblance of a throne
he'll ever know, and lays in
for the cut, the counseling of
older dudes, cappin' players, men-of-words,
Greek chorus to the comic-tragic fanfare
of approaching manhood.

Baby brother's named for two fathers,
and each Saturday he seeks them
in this neutral zone of brotherhood,
where manhood sprouts like new growth
week by week and dark hands
deftly shape identity.

Head-bowed, church-solemn,
he sheds hair like motherlove & virginity,
weightier than Air Jordans & designer
sweats — euphemistic battle gear.
He receives the tribal standard:
a nappy helmet sporting arrows, lightning
bolts, rows of lines cut in — New World
scarification — or carved logos (Adidas,
Public Enemy) and tags, like hieroglyphic
distress signs to the ancestors:
Remember us, remember our names!

Angela Jackson

....

CHOOSING THE BLUES
(for S. Brandi Barnes)

When Willie Mae went down to the barber shop
to visit her boyfriend who cut hair there
I went with her. Walking beside her on the street
the men said hey and stopped to watch her just walk.
Boyfriend Barber cut hair and cut his glance at her
O, he could see the tree for the forest. He pressed
down the wild crest on a man's head and shaved it off
just so he could watch her standing there by the juke
box choosing the blues she would wear for the afternoon.
Right there Little Milton would shoot through the store-
front with the peppermint stick sentry twirling outside
"If I didn't love you, baby, grits ain't groceries, eggs
ain't poultry and Mona Lisa was a man."
And every razor and mouth would stop its dissembling
business. And Time sit down in the barber's chair
and tell Memory poised with its scissors in hand
not to cut it too short, just take a little off the ends.

Kevin Young

....

EDDIE PRIEST'S BARBERSHOP & NOTARY
Closed Mondays

is music   is men
off early from work   is waiting
for the chance at the chair
while the eagle claws holes
in your pockets   keeping
time   by the turning
of rusty fans   steel flowers with
cold breezes   is having nothing
better to do   than guess at the years
of hair   matted beneath the soiled caps
of drunks   the pain of running
a fisted comb through stubborn
knots   is the dark dirty low
down blues   the tender heads
of sons fresh from cornrows   all
wonder at losing   half their height
is a mother gathering hair   for good
luck   for a soft wig   is the round
difficulty of ears   the peach
faced boys asking Eddie
to cut in parts and arrows
wanting to have their names read
for just a few days   and among thin
jazz   is the quick brush of a done
head   and the black flood around
your feet   the grandfathers
stopping their games of ivory
dominoes   just before they reach the bone
yard   is winking widowers announcing
cut it clean off   I'm through courting
and hair only gets in the way   is the final
spin of the chair   a reflection of
a reflection   that sting of wintergreen
tonic   on the neck of a sleeping snow
haired man   when you realize it is
your turn   you are next

INITIATION

1.

Porch sitting hairbraiding
full of whys
questions for the faith
the rush of childtimes
slows the crafting of old hands
she wrangles my thickness into design
impatient arrows to the sun
fire from my head
the pull and rock of her ways
brings me back
done
she sends me out
the arrows reach
pull my back straight
i walk like a heron
clouds beneath my feet
looking into the sun
yellow becomes circles
circles bring out the creatures
zooming inside my eyes
the creatures make me dizzy
the sun puts me to sleep.

2.

i watch
woman circle approaching
black swans fly
trees bend
it rains mercury
my body burns   reddens
the women bear knives
the rain comes clear
the redness chases
down my thighs into the ground
woman circle bends to me

they rub my stomach
they cut my skin
singing
circles comin like the moon
test you for your tribal tune
circles tighten round and play
water seasons what we pay
bear it gently like the earth
rivers twist and give us birth
don't forget her blue black hand
the love knots in your hair the land
deny the knowledge grow your fears
the pain will last for all our years.

3.

humming they move away
i am a giant
my braids are many rivers
my toes curl round mountain peaks
the night comes
pours into me
slow-moving and warm
the warmth moves me like a dancer
i am filled to dawning
i am small again.

4.

porchsitting childwaiting
she rubs my stomach
we swing together
the pull rock and push bring me back
her fingers explore
the licorice roots in my hair
her head finds a home on my shoulder
the sun puts her to sleep
she is small again.

Michelle T. Clinton

....

EVICTION

White men handed papers to my mother
through a cracked door. We had to
get boxes from the liquor store
& watch her get drunk.

Before, just yesterday, my mother
brought home purple heart doilies
& gave us large silver coins
we held tight in our hands
running to catch ice cream bells.

Yesterday she baked macaroons,
she talked to her plants & scrubbed
even the air with her sure, careful
movements. Now she sits. She stares;
she drinks.

And after our disassembled home,
rum, gin, & vodka boxes are carried
on the backs of large & small men
swarming about my mother's drunken
laughter.

After the doilies have been gathered,
the plants limp with root shock
are placed on the orange U-Haul,

We will jump on beds &
throw kung fu kicks at the walls,
We will break windows & shriek
as they shatter, for the unyielding blue eyes,
the unknown, untouchable Authority
that disrupted
this, the peace
of my mother's home.

Yusef Komunyakaa

WHITE PORT AND LEMON JUICE

At fifteen I'd buy bottles
& hide them inside a drainpipe
Behind the school
Before Friday-night football.
Nothing was as much fun
As shouldering a guard
To the ground on the snap,
& we could only be destroyed
By another boy's speed
On the twenty-yard line.

Up the middle on two, Joe.
Eddie Earl, you hit that damn
Right tackle, & don't let those
Cheerleaders take your eyes off
The ball. We knew the plays
But little about biology
& what we remembered about
French
Was a flicker of blue lace
When the teacher crossed her legs.

Our City of Lights
Glowed when they darkened
The field at halftime
& a hundred freejack girls
Marched with red & green pen-
lights
Fastened to their white boots
As the brass band played
"It Don't Mean A Thing."
They stepped so high.
The air tasted like jasmine.

We'd shower & rub
Ben-Gay into our muscles
Till the charley horses
Left. Girls would wait
Among the lustrous furniture
Of shadows, ready to
Sip white port & lemon juice.
Music from the school dance
Pulsed through our bodies
As we leaned against the brick wall:

Ernie K-Doe, Frogman
Henry, The Dixie Cups, & Little Richard.
Like echo chambers,
We'd du-wop song after song
& hold the girls in rough arms,
Not knowing they didn't want to be
Embraced with the strength
We used against fullbacks
& tight ends on the fifty.

Sometimes they rub against us,
Preludes to failed flesh,
Trying to kiss defeat
From our eyes. The fire
Wouldn't catch. We tried
To dodge the harvest moon
That grew red through trees,
In our Central High gold-
&-blue jackets, with perfect
Cleat marks on the skin.

Pinkie Gordon Lane
....
RAIN DITCH

We swam in the rain-filled gully
one day
three black kids
unmindful of death's spectre:
water snakes
fever
cow dung floating like a drowned corpse,
the level of that ditch
our shoulders' height,
the water to our asses.

And just over the hill the weeds
bowed like cloistered nuns at vespers.
At eye distance just beyond,
our house's top formed a gray peak
against a crimson sky.

We remembered our fun for days,
talked about it,
longed for another torrent of rain
so that we could splash again in that
death trap.

Etheridge Knight
....
THE IDEA OF ANCESTRY

I
Taped to the wall of my cell are 47 pictures: 47 black
faces: my father, mother, grandmothers (1 dead), grand-
fathers (both dead), brothers, sisters, uncles, aunts,
cousins (1st & 2nd), nieces, and nephews. They stare
across the space at me sprawling on my bunk. I know
their dark eyes, they know mine. I know their style,
they know mine. I am all of them, they are all of me;
they are farmers, I am a thief, I am me, they are thee.

I have at one time or another been in love with my mother
1 grandmother, 2 sisters, 2 aunts (1 went to the asylum),
and 5 cousins. I am now in love with a 7 yr old niece
(she sends me letters written in large block print, and
her picture is the only one that smiles at me).

I have the same name as 1 grandfather, 3 cousins, 3 nephews,
and 1 uncle. The uncle disappeared when he was 15, just took
off and caught a freight (they say). He's discussed each year
when the family has a reunion, he causes uneasiness in
the clan, he is an empty space. My father's mother, who is 93
and who keeps the Family Bible with everybody's birth dates
(and death dates) in it, always mentions him. There is no
place in her Bible for "whereabouts unknown."

2
Each fall the graves of my grandfathers call me, the brown
hills and red gullies of mississippi send out their electric
messages, galvanizing my genes. Last yr / like a salmon quitting
the cold ocean—leaping and bucking up his birthstream / I
hitchhiked my way from L.A. with 16 caps in my pocket and a
monkey on my back. And I almost kicked it with the kinfolks.
I walked barefooted in my grandmother's backyard / I smelled the old
land and the woods / I sipped cornwhiskey from fruit jars with the men /
I flirted with the women / I had a ball till the caps ran out
and my habit came down. That night I looked at my grandmother
and split / my guts were screaming for junk / but I was almost
contented / I had almost caught up with me.
(The next day in Memphis I cracked a croaker's crib for a fix.)

This yr there is a gray stone wall damming my stream, and when
the falling leaves stir my genes, I pace my cell or flop on my bunk
and stare at the 47 black faces across the space. I am all of them,
they are all of me, I am me, they are thee, and I have no children
to float in the space between.

lamont b. steptoe
....
O' YES

O' yes
good citizens
workers in factories
workers in mines
workers in offices
workers working to eat
to sleep to work again
it is your dollars
your tax dollars
that have purchased these moments

Cornelius Eady
....
SUCCESS

I will stop dreaming now
now that I've finally made it.
outside I can hear the wind
rustling through the leaves of trees.
I own those trees.

Lucille Clifton
....
GOOD TIMES

My Daddy has paid the rent
and the insurance man is gone
and the lights is back on
and my uncle Brud has hit
for one dollar straight
and they is good times
good times
good times

My Mama has made bread
and Grampaw has come
and everybody is drunk
and dancing in the kitchen
and singing in the kitchen
oh these is good times
good times
good times

oh children think about the
good times

HEALING POEMS

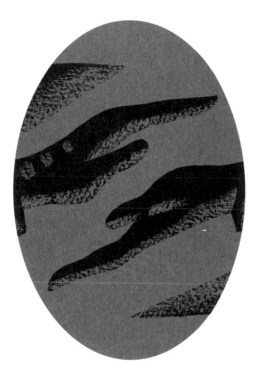

Adesanya Alakoye
....
ESHU

I will whisper your name
on the winds of each new sun
to carry my prayers to you
and you
mischief maker
lord of chance
will place my words
at the feet of
oludumare . . .

Langston Hughes
....
FEET O' JESUS

At the feet o' Jesus,
Sorrow like a sea.
Lordy, let yo' mercy
Come driftin' down on me.

At the feet o' Jesus
At yo' feet I stand.
O, ma little Jesus,
Please reach out yo' hand.

Thomas A. Dorsey

....

TAKE MY HAND, PRECIOUS LORD

Precious Lord, take my hand,
Lead me on, let me stand,
I am tired, I am weak, I am worn.
Through the storm, through the night
Lead me on to the light,
Take my hand, precious Lord,
Lead me home.

When my way grows drear,
Precious Lord, linger near.
When my life is almost gone,
Hear my cry, hear my call,
Hold my hand lest I fall.
Take my hand, precious Lord,
Lead me home.

When the darkness appears
And the night draws near,
And the day is past and gone,
At the river I stand,
Guide my feet, hold my hand.
Take my hand, precious Lord
Lead me home.

Owen Dodson

....

BLACK MOTHER PRAYING

My great God, You been a tenderness to me,
Through the thick and through the thin;
You been a pilla to my soul;
You been like the shinin light a mornin in the black dark,
A elevator to my spirit.

Now there's a fire in this land like a last judgment,
And I done sat down by the rivers of Babylon
And wept deep when I remembered Zion,
Seein the water that can't quench fire
And the fire that burn up rivers.
Lord, I'm gonna say my say real quick and simple:

You know bout this war that's bitin the skies and gougin out the earth.
Last month, Lord, I bid my last boy away to fight.
I got all my boys fightin now for they country.
Didn't think bout it cept it were for freedom;
Didn't think cause they was black they wasn't American;
Didn't think a thing cept that they was my only sons,
And there was mothers all over the world
Sacrificin they sons like You let Yours be nailed
To the wood for men to behold the right.

Now I'm a black mother, Lord, I knows that now,
Black and burnin in these burnin times.
I can't hold my peace cause peace ain't fit to mention
When they's fightin right here in our streets
Like dogs—mongrel dogs and hill cats.
White is fightin black right here where hate abides like a cancer wound
And Freedom is writ big and crossed out:
Where, bless God, they's draggin us outta cars
In Texas and California, in Newark, Detroit.

Blood on the darkness, Lord, blood on the pavement,
Leavin us moanin and afraid.
What has we done?
Where and when has we done?
They's plantin the seeds of hate down in our bone marrow
When we don't want to hate.

We don't speak much in the street where I live, my God,
Nobody speak much, but we thinkin deep
Of the black sons in lands far as the wind can go,
Black boys fightin this war with them.

We thinkin deep bout they sisters stitchin airplane canvas,
And they old fathers plowin for wheat,
And they mothers bendin over washtubs,
They brothers at the factory wheels:
They all is bein body beat and spirit beat and heart sore and wonderin.

Listen, Lord, they ain't nowhere for black mothers to turn.
Won't You plant Your Son's goodness in this land
Before it too late?
Set Your stars of sweetness twinklin over us like winda lamps
Before it too late?
Help these men to see they losin while they winnin
Long as they allow theyselves to lynch in the city streets and on country roads?

When can I pray again,
View peace in my own parlor again?
When my sons come home
How can I show em my broken hands?
How can I show em they sister's twisted back?
How can I present they land to them?
How, when they been battlin in far places for freedom?
Better let em die in the desert drinkin sand
Or holdin onto water and shippin into death
Than they come back an see they sufferin for vain.

I done seen a man runnin for his life,
Runnin like the wind from a mob, to no shelter.
Where were a hidin place for him?
Saw a dark girl nine years old
Cryin cause her father done had
The light scratched from his eyes in the month of June.
Where the seein place for him?
A black boy lyin with his arms huggin the pavement in pain.
What he starin at?
Good people hands up, searched for guns and razors and pipes.
When they gonna pray again?

How, precious God, can I watch my sons' eyes
When they hear this terrible?
How can I pray again when my tongue
Is near cleavin to the roof of my mouth?
Tell me, Lord, how?

Every time they strike us, they strikin Your Son;
Every time they shove us in, they cornerin they own children.
I'm gonna scream before I hope again.
I ain't never gonna hush my mouth or lay down this heavy, black,
    weary, terrible load
Until I fights to stamp my feet with my black sons
On a freedom solid rock and stand there peaceful
And look out into the star wilderness of the sky
And the land lyin about clean, and secure land,
And people not afraid again.

Lord, let us all see the golden wheat together,
Harvest the harvest together,
Touch the fulness and the hallelujah together.
                                        Amen.

Michael S. Weaver

WATER SONG

In the house that has died,
the dead come down wooden stairs at noon,
puffing the cotton curtain, a cramped bunch
of light pressing down step by step burning,
stopping at the dining room, sitting on
plastic table covers, circling the window,
then they jet through the empty mansion
chasing each other, embracing the empty space
where granddaddy's picture was kept until
the fall from grace, the deaths in the water,
the water of the lake all around the house,
holding the life still there at siege,
jealous mirrors bobbing on small waves that
swallow and fill the lungs with screaming.

No man knows his time, but his time is appointed.

The slipshod mules with box heads and flies,
collars and reins worn to brown frazzle and fiber,
darkened and hardened corn scattered in feed bins,
an empty smokehouse with padlock opened and rusted,
covered outhouse dumps sinking, the old house
flapping its open door back and forth admitting,
garden patch aside going broke under weeds and snakes,
the backporch where we bathed and pinched the girls,
a victorian mansion of wood and tin and screens,
its skin thinning, its bones going hollow and ashen,
its mind blossoming out and over the farm, growing.
Down the path behind the corn crib there is still
the crack of bushes beneath his feet, fallen pine
branches snapping under the crush of his hands,
the restless moan of the mules bemoaning his call,
his call away, the intonation of angels in his ears,
coming down to turn the home into an ugly wailing,
there is still the flailing of arms in lake water,
armies of people in the abandoned home, discarnate.

The dead come back to old folk in the country to talk.

·········

An empty swirl of leaves, empty but for the ghosts,
has fallen in through the window, swirling on the floor,
bronze, yellow gold, black, crisp as paper,
popping up and down on gray, painted floors,
the lives take hold and breathe in the decay,
travelling down the hallway where grandma slept,
gushed by sudden air into the living room where
summer visitors from up north slept and whispered,
back into the kitchen against the hard iron legs
of the stove, they dance and shout echoes,
a shudder in the house and they are gone back,
following evening rays back to the sun, sucking
back to the moon at night, instant glitter
on the roof, then nothing but dull tin and
the evening gossip of angels when the lake
slaps a wet tongue on muddy banks and steep falls.

In the twinkling of an eye, in the twinkling of an eye.

Homemade brooms of straw, bundles wrapped in twine,
skirting the wooden floor, scraping the rough finish,
hands dipping into white, metal wash basins, cupped
in prayer, rubbing against faces grimy with oil,
headless chickens tied to upturned poles, flapping
their wings in anger, feathers filling the yard,
hogs grunting over slop, sleeping in their food,
a pair of hands operating the udder of the cow,
raw milk spraying against the bucket in squirts,
bowl upon bowl of hot vegetables toted to the table,
pot-bellied stove churning an inferno of wood,
in the house that has died and is decaying,
there is laughter, prayer, singing, cursing,
the blare of radios, inordinate snoring from a farmer
who sang his own eulogy as he walked to the lake,
sirens like Egyptian handmaidens over the deepest
move of waves, Canaan in the splashing of catfish,
in the house that has died and is decaying, a shell
of a place where people no longer live in flesh.

Death holds no fear for folk who are Christians.

....

Grandma sits on the back porch in a metal glider,
riding silently back and forth, cobwebs in the corner,
Her spittoon from a Campbell's soup can
by her foot, through the door comes a sucking
energy like a giant, empty heart with open arms.
She goes again back into the mist of it with
all of them, all the blood of the farm that
has gone to the water and all the plethora
of death, all the endless ways of leaving
in the air over the farm, among the million
blades of grass pushing up, in the clearings
between the pines, a harsh crackle from c.b. radios,
an ambulance starting up from the lake weighed
by a sudden journey to Canaan, through and past
the lake. The life slips free over the fields.

I will be back in the by and by. Dying ain't forever.

In the house that has died,
the dead come down wooden stairs at midnight,
soft feet like cotton shuffling to the front porch,
sitting down to dangle over the edge, examining
the picnic table where children ate watermelon.
Granddaddy sits in his corner, napping, sleeping
in the nest of a big, empty heart, a sucking energy,
a song like Egyptian handmaidens over the lake,
the dark, moving silence around this world.

Yusef Komunyakaa

MY FATHER'S LOVELETTERS

On Fridays he'd open a can of Jax
After coming home from the mill,
& ask me to write a letter to my mother
Who sent postcards of desert flowers
Taller than men. He would beg,
Promising to never beat her
Again. Somehow I was happy
She had gone, & sometimes wanted
To slip in a reminder, how Mary Lou
Williams's "Polka Dots & Moonbeams"
Never made the swelling go down.
His carpenter's apron always bulged
With old nails, a claw hammer
Looped at his side & extension cords
Coiled around his feet.
Words rolled from under the pressure
Of my ballpoint: Love,
Baby, Honey, Please.

We sat in the quiet brutality
Of voltage meters & pipe threaders,
Lost between sentences . . .
The gleam of a five-pound wedge
On the concrete floor
Pulled a sunset
Through the doorway of his toolshed.
I wondered if she laughed
& held them over a gas burner.
My father could only sign
His name, but he'd look at blueprints
& say how many bricks
Formed each wall. This man,
Who stole roses & hyacinth
For his yard, would stand there
With eyes closed & fists balled,
Laboring over a simple word, almost
Redeemed by what he tried to say.

Jacquie Jones

DRUGS

he slept in my bed
i felt him in the dark
i knew his breathing
i loved him

this was no war
we were in college

and smoking coke
was like smoking dope
in the 60s

only it wasn't

he stole my camera and my money
he stopped sleeping
he touched the side of my face
with the side of a gun

they came at night
they kicked in my door
metal hung from their belts
and from their chests

this was a war
they said

they threw my books
on the floor

and people like him
were the enemy
they said

they were the good guys

and what was a nice girl like me
doing mixed up
in this anyhow

honey didn't i know
these guys would do anything
for it

one of them touched me

he slept in my bed
they kicked in my door
i felt him in the dark
they called me honey
i knew his breathing
didn't i know

they would do
anything

E. Ethelbert Miller
....
REBECCA

will i hate mirrors?
will i hate reflections?
will i hate to dress?
will i hate to undress?

jim my husband
tells me it won't matter
if i have one or two
two or one it doesn't matter
he says

but it does
i know it does

this is my body
this is not south africa or nicaragua

this is my body
losing a war against cancer
and there are no demonstrators outside
the hospital to scream stop

there is only jim
sitting in the lobby
wondering what to say
the next time we love
and his hands move towards
my one surviving breast

how do we convince ourselves
it doesn't matter?
how do i embrace my own nakedness
now that it is no longer complete?

Gwendolyn Brooks

··········

THE MOTHER

Abortions will not let you forget.
You remember the children you got that you did not get,
The damp small pulps with a little or with no hair,
The singers and workers that never handled the air.
You will never neglect or beat
Them, or silence or buy with a sweet.
You will never wind up the sucking-thumb
Or scuttle off ghosts that come.
You will never leave them, controlling your luscious sigh,
Return for a snack of them, with gobbling mother-eye.

I have heard in the voices of the wind the voices of my dim
    killed children.
I have contracted. I have eased
My dim dears at the breasts they could never suck.
I have said, Sweets, if I sinned, if I seized
Your luck
And your lives from your unfinished reach,
If I stole your births and your names,
Your straight baby tears and your games,
Your stilted or lovely loves, your tumults, your
    marriages, aches, and your deaths,
If I poisoned the beginnings of your breaths,
Believe that even in my deliberateness I was not deliberate.
Though why should I whine,
Whine that the crime was other than mine?—
Since anyhow you are dead.
Or rather, or instead,
You were never made.

But that too, I am afraid,
Is faulty: oh, what shall I say, how is the truth to be said?
You were born, you had body, you died.
It is just that you never giggled or planned or cried.

Believe me, I loved you all.
Believe me, I knew you, though faintly, and I loved, I loved you
All.

Lucille Clifton

. . . .

THE LOST BABY POEM

the time i dropped your almost body down
down to meet the waters under the city
and run one with the sewage to the sea
what did i know about waters rushing back
what did i know about drowning
or being drowned

you would have been born into winter
in the year of the disconnected gas
and no car   we would have made the thin
walk over Genesee hill into the Canada wind

to watch you slip like ice into strangers' hands
you would have fallen naked as snow into winter
if you were here i could tell you these
and some other things

if i am ever less than a mountain
for your definite brothers and sisters
let the rivers pour over my head
let the sea take me for a spiller
of seas   let black men call me stranger
always   for your never named sake

Calvin Forbes

. . . .

PICTURE OF A MAN

He draws a man,
bright swirls of red.
And I say give me a tree.
He points to the middle
of his red and says
"there's a tree!"
Tonight without complaining
he goes off to sleep
asking why in his story book
the big boats have little
boats. He shouts
goodnight: I ask if he wants
the lights out—

he says no, that he can't see
without the light.
A different excuse than
last night when he was plain scared.
Later I turn off the light—
his face soft as a breast.
And I know then what another man
meant when he said
maybe I could have loved
better
but I couldn't have loved more.
I thought of a woman
like that once.
This child is all I have left.

Kenneth Carroll
....

THE TRUTH ABOUT KAREN

in our kitchen,
brown women are whispering
i am not supposed to hear
i listened.
it is about karen
about ambulances
secrets, taboos
"women thangs"
the heartbreak of mothers

i was not supposed to hear
i listened.
karen had almost died
had almost bled to death in a bathroom
the coat hanger's jagged tip rested
near her bare feet
across the courtyard the temprees sang,
"explain it to her mama"

i was not supposed to know these things
i huddled quietly, invisibly near the hallway
heard the brown women whisper, painful & rhythmic
karen's mama had not explained any of it
karen at 17 could not explain it to her mama
but someone had told karen about the old ways
home remedies, old wives tales
dangerous as ignorance

karen could not tell her mama
stood alone in the bathroom
stood alone in the world
quietly groping with metal inside her
desperately hoping to avoid the cyclical
error of her mother
of babies as ball & chains

....

i was not supposed to hear this stuff
soft spoken horrors of oppression & despair
i wished i had not
karen stood in her own blood
as it puddled at her feet
blindly jabbing herself
tears falling in torrents
testament to unbearable pain
but where was the water?
the shadow voices had promised this would work
the pain too was foretold,
but where was the water to signal an end
to keep karen from turning to/into her mother
whose face she could not stand in this condition
whose heart she was sure to break with this unspeakable truth
in the courtyard the "whatnots" sang,
"i'll erase away your pain"

i was not supposed to hear
i listened.
now wishing i had not
the water never came
the ambulance did
they saved karen from a bloody drowning
what she could not tell her mother,
soon everyone would know
a trail of blood stains littered the sidewalk
i followed them to the curb
prayed for a cleansing rain to wash them all away
the whispers talked of pints lost
hospitals, shame, babies, welfare
the boy & the boy's family
of circles, viciously accurate & unending

the kitchen whispers,
i was not supposed to hear,
did not know of the school-boy crush
i wore for karen
of how i burned in a pubescent flame at her sight
of how quickly 13 year old hearts crumble

silently i crumbled in a teary heap,
hands pressed violently against my ears,
the whispered words exploding like sirens
my back slammed against a painted cinderblock wall
as the truth about karen stole the innocence from my soul
puncturing my heart like the bloody jagged edge of oppression

that summer
love songs raged in the courtyard
as young lovers held each other
slow dragged along a razor's edge
as if the truth about karen was not known

i avoided karen's eyes
marveled at her bulging form
wondered how she could smile
cursed the whispered voices,
the truth,
& love.

James Weldon Johnson
....

GO DOWN DEATH

Weep not, weep not,
She is not dead;
She's resting in the bosom of Jesus.
Heart-broken husband—weep no more;
Grief-stricken son—weep no more;
She's only just gone home.

Day before yesterday morning,
God was looking down from his great, high heaven,
Looking down on all his children,
And his eye fell on Sister Caroline,
Tossing on her bed of pain.
And God's big heart was touched with pity,
With the everlasting pity.

And God sat back on his throne,
And he commanded that tall, bright angel standing at his right hand:
Call me Death!
And that tall, bright angel cried in a voice
That broke like a clap of thunder:
Call Death!—Call Death!
And the echo sounded down the streets of heaven
Till it reached away back to that shadowy place,
Where Death waits with his pale, white horses.

And Death heard the summons,
And he leaped on his fastest horse,
Pale as a sheet in the moonlight.
Up the golden street Death galloped,
And the hoof of his horse struck fire from the gold,
But they didn't make no sound.
Up Death rode to the Great White Throne,
And waited for God's command.

And God said: Go down, Death, go down,
Go down to Savannah, Georgia,
Down in Yamacraw,
And find Sister Caroline.
She's borne the burden and heat of the day,
She's labored long in my vineyard,
And she's tired—
She's weary—
Go down, Death, and bring her to me.

And Death didn't say a word,
But he loosed the reins on his pale, white horse,
And he clamped the spurs to his bloodless sides,
And out and down he rode,
Through heaven's pearly gates,
Past suns and moons and stars;
On Death rode,
And the foam from his horse was like a comet in the sky;
On Death rode,
Leaving the lightning's flash behind;
Straight on down he came.

While we were watching round her bed,
She turned her eyes and looked away,
She saw what we couldn't see;
She saw Old Death. She saw Old Death.
Coming like a falling star.
But Death didn't frighten Sister Caroline;
He looked to her like a welcome friend.
And she whispered to us; I'm going home,
And she smiled and closed her eyes.

And Death took her up like a baby,
And she lay in his icy arms,
But she didn't feel no chill.
And Death began to ride again—
Up beyond the evening star,
Out beyond the morning star,
Into the glittering light of glory,
On to the Great White Throne.
And there he laid Sister Caroline
On the loving breast of Jesus.

And Jesus took his own hand and wiped away her tears
And he smoothed the furrows from her face,
And the angels sang a little song,
And Jesus rocked her in his arms,
And kept a-saying: Take your rest,
Take your rest, take your rest.
Weep not—weep not,
She is not dead;
She's resting in the bosom of Jesus.

Alice Walker

....

"GOOD NIGHT, WILLIE LEE, I'LL SEE YOU IN THE MORNING"

Looking down into my father's
dead face
for the last time
my mother said without
tears, without smiles
without regrets
but with *civility*
"Good night, Willie Lee, I'll see you
in the morning."
And it was then I knew that the healing
of all our wounds
is forgiveness
that permits a promise
of our return
at the end.

Houston A. Baker, Jr.

....

TOWARD GUINEA: FOR LARRY NEAL, 1937-1981

I remember your strut.
Disguised as Garvey's ghost,
You entered the room.
Your plumed stride and narrow eyes
Matched the peacock's radiant glory.
You gave the shout of Shine,
Bellowed like James Brown,
Swam miraculously against white currents.
And now you have left . . .

Tomorrow's dawn will find you moving toward Guinea:
Jamming again on African ground,
A bright reunion
Of ancestral sound.

WHEN THE SAINTS GO MARCHING IN

When the saints go marching in
When the saints go marching in
I want to be in that number
When the saints go marching in.

I used to have some playmates
Who used to play with me.
But since I've been converted
They done turned their backs on me.

Oh, when they crown Him Lord of Lords
Oh, when they crown Him Lord of Lords
Yes, I want to be in that number
When they crown Him Lord of Lords.

When they march all around His throne
When they march all around His throne.
Oh, I want to be in that number
When they march all around His throne.

I have a dear old mother who has gone on before
And left me here below,
But I know I'm gonna meet her
When the saints go marchin in.

When the saints go marching in,
Oh, when the saints go marching in!
Oh, Lord I want to be in that number
When the saints go marching in.

Eugene B. Redmond

....

POETIC REFLECTIONS ENROUTE TO, AND DURING, THE FUNERAL AND BURIAL OF HENRY DUMAS, POET

I

FLIGHT TO NEW YORK

> *"I am ready to die"*
> — Henry Dumas in
> *"Our King Is Dead,"* 1968.

A passive sea of white foam
Separates this swift and fleshless bird
From the black earth that waits for *Henry Dumas, poet.*
At 30,000 feet up
The mind has plenty of space to wander:

Just think!
A second-story world—
No steps, no ladders.
Meanwhile onto aluminum-covered wings the sun leaps
And breaks into a thousand heated needles
As my head averts,
With a twist,
Its stabbing, staring presence.

Now we soar through angry winds,
Bouncing unpredictably like a football
Turned loose in some smooth, open place.
But the pilot guides the bird cautiously
Through the ordeal while our hearts,
At first hung like anxious medallions around our necks,
Resume their natural places;
And the cries, before dignifiedly choked,
Die forever in our throats.

We the living:
Are we some majestic, royal party?
A high tribunal judging the lower world?
Gods? Goddesses?
Who is above and who is below?
. . . the pilot's voice and then
A view of Staten Island.

·········

We nose through the second sea to caress LaGuardia Field.
The stewardess smiles at the passenger sitting
Alone in the rear: "Pretty good landing in the rain, wasn't it?"
She's a company girl, the poet muses—a robot with nice legs.
Parts and rhythms of the painful puzzle fall together on the ground.
But I must hurry to the funeral in the Bronx.
Amid sounds and sights, I near the cab and am terrified at my image
In the glossy surface of its wet body.

And on the way to McCall Funeral Home
I try in vain to figure out who I am.

II
THE FUNERAL

"A Black Poet is a preacher."
—Statement by Henry Dumas, 1968

The balding black preacher
Read and ad-libbed
Before a lamp that threw
A cone-shaped light up into his face.
The eulogy was brief,
The man was eloquent and magnificent
In dark robes: *a poet saluting a poet.*
Occasionally his eyes fell
Like heavy weights
On the casket to his right,
Draped in a United States flag.
Dumas had served in the Air Force.
The articulate preacher had not known the poet
But the poet's mother.
One could see that the circumstances of the killing
Had undermined his faith.

He sought a way out: Equating the poet with "Mr.
   Lincoln."
He also knew the poet wrote:
"This young man will survive
In his stories and poems," the bowed audience was
Reminded.
"He walked upright like a man . . .
There are mysteries; life is a mystery,

Death is a mystery."
The radiant black man of cloth
Was unpretentious; he broke with tradition—promising
No alternatives to death.
Seemingly unaware of heaven or hell, he suggested simply "a last **resting place**."
Those in the chapel stared intently, bleakly
Into their own thoughts.
Outside the skies cried for the dead black bard.

III
FORTY-FIVE MINUTES TO THE CEMETERY

Rain,
Earlier in East St. Louis and now in New York.
The skies continue to mourn for the fallen poet and warrior,
Mojo-handler and prophet.

Four passengers in the fourth car,
Divided by a generation of intellect,
But feeling a common pain,
A mutual bewilderment:
Four grit faces of the oppressed.

The dead poet rode in the first car
But was present in the whole train:
Smiling in approval at our candid talk.
Dumas was like that. "Man, let's just tell it," he used to say.
Yes, and he had given direction to the
Pen of the younger poet earlier that morning
Several stories up, adrift in a big bird of steel.

Our talk was shop:
"Henry and I finished Commerce High School together,"
The driver intimated.
A middleage friend of the poet's mother said:
"They're killing off all our good men; I tell ya, a black man
Today speaks his piece at the risk of losing his life."

New Yorkers talk differently than East St. Louisans,
The younger poet observed to himself.

The cars of the procession,
Standing out with bright eyes against the dim day,

Sped cautiously toward Farmingdale National Cemetery
Where white marble headstones stood mute and macabre:
Quite geometrically arranged in a sprawling well kept ocean of green.

Again talk: "They're slaughtering our boys in Vietnam," the middleage lady
Quipped; "this graveyard will be filled up soon."
A bus carrying the Army Honor Guard joined us at the entrance to the cemetery.

The guard gave a trifling, sloppy salute to the fallen poet
Who had served his country.
More talk as we departed the graveside:
"Young David walks just like his daddy,"
The driver informed us about Dumas' eldest son.

"Neither of the boys understand what's going on,"
The driver's mother noted.
"Who does?" the young poet asked himself.

A confession from the middleage lady: "Can't cry no more.
Just won't no more tears come out—all dried up."
Her eyes looked like worn rubies, inquisitive jewels
Polished to worn perfection
By having seen many things
Including the dead poet's "good looking"
Remains.
The driver echoed her: "Henry was beautiful; he looked
Just like he was asleep."

The driver was a spirit lifter, also an interior observer:
"Henry thought too deep for the average person."

Upon leaving the cemetery
The procession broke up.
Cars bearing license plates from various places sped on or turned off,
Went their way and my way.

The skies lifted their hung heads.
Mrs. Dumas smiled finally and played with her sons,
David and Michael.
The boys, cast in the same physical mold as their father,
Were impeccably dressed.

May Miller

A CLOSING

In a house of empty rooms
I thought I heard a door close
down the long hall.
I couldn't know
whether someone had entered,
whether someone had left.
No further step,
simply the closing of a door—
an absence of other defined stir,
more like the hum of water
in a hidden spring,
like a starved echo
from an exacting hill
I could not measure.
I reached for the reassuring hand.
It was not there.
He had gone ahead.

OUR WORLD IS LESS FULL NOW THAT MR. FULLER IS GONE

It is always difficult to measure
and certainly impossible to replace
the vital space
that a friend's
final passage leaves

At the funeral site
i viewed the corpse
—and that is what that was,
the man we knew
was not lying there
silent, still and accepting
of circumstance
that was never Hoyt
striding, stirring, agitating —

From somewhere
Hoyt's death reached me
the evening of the notice
of Marley's dying, i remembered
i muttered an obscenity,
the certainty of death
for us all does nothing
to lessen the impact
when fighters fall
however, it is our way
that only the forgotten are
truly dead, the remembered
live always inside of us
simply moved to another
plane of existence

I know it is an appropriate
occasion for brilliant phrases
and praise poems
describing his work
and worth, but i don't
feel that right
now, as i watch writers
relatives and friends
view the remains
sadness aches my head
and tastes dry in my mouth
Let us transform this touching grief
before we return to the front
(and hopefully that is where
we all are
headed from here),
let us work as hard as he
stopping only at the
time of our going,
let us retain his memory
chew it like mint
swallow and make muscle of it
and resolve to each of us
secure a portion and create Hoyt
whole again rising within
the community
of our carrying on

Sterling A. Brown

....

SISTER LOU

Honey
When de man
Calls out de las' train
You're gonna ride,
Tell him howdy.

Gather up yo' basket
An' yo' knittin' an' yo' things,
An' go on up an' visit
Wid frien' Jesus fo' a spell.

Show Marfa
How to make yo' greengrape jellies,
An' give po' Lazarus
A passel of them Golden Biscuits.

Scald some meal
Fo' some righdown good spoonbread
Fo' li'l box-plunkin' David.

An' sit aroun'
An' tell them Hebrew Chillen
All yo' stories. . . .

Honey
Don't be feared of them pearly gates,
Don't go 'round to de back,
No mo' dataway
Not evah no mo'.

Let Michael tote yo' burden
An' yo' pocketbook an' evahthing
'Cept yo' Bible,
While Gabriel blows somp'n
Solemn but loudsome
On dat horn of his'n.

Honey
Go straight on to de Big House,
An' speak to yo' God
Widout no fear an' tremblin'.

Then sit down
An' pass de time of day awhile.

Give a good talkin' to
To yo' favorite 'postle Peter,
An' rub the po' head
Of mixed-up Judas,
An' joke awhile wid Jonah.

Then, when you gits de chance,
Always rememberin' yo' raisin',
Let 'em know youse tired
Jest a mite tired.

Jesus will find yo' bed fo' you
Won't no servant evah bother wid yo' room.
Jesus will lead you
To a room wid windows
Openin' on cherry trees an' plum trees
Bloomin' everlastin'.

An' dat will be yours
Fo' keeps.

Den take yo' time. . . .
Honey, take yo' bressed time.

Jerry W. Ward, Jr.
....
COMFORT-MAKER
(for Toni Morrison)

on a needful day
your terribleness troubles

the house like thunderclaps
ripping a Delta sky.

You gather a bushel of autumn,
run faithfilled fingers over your threads.

Your needles of sunlight
worry a healing into history.

The ancient lady in your bones
memories out the quilts.

Her leafwork stitches spring
invisible at the seams.

You know winter starwars
have designs to freeze our flesh.

Your preternatural covers
blithely summer us into dawn.

Bob Kaufman
....
PRIVATE SADNESS

Sitting here alone, in peace
With my private sadness
Bared of the acquirements
Of the mind's eye
Vision reversed, upended,
Seeing only the holdings
Inside the walls of me,
Feeling the roots that bind me,
To this mere human tree
Thrashing to free myself,
Knowing the success
Of these burstings
Shall be measured
By the fury
Of the fall
To eternal peace
The end of All.

Dudley Randall

....

BALLAD OF BIRMINGHAM
(On the Bombing of a Church in Birmingham, Alabama, 1963)

"Mother dear, may I go downtown
Instead of out to play,
And march the streets of Birmingham
In a Freedom March today?"

"No, baby, no, you may not go,
For the dogs are fierce and wild,
And clubs and hoses, guns and jail
Aren't good for a little child."

"But, mother, I won't be alone.
Other children will go with me,
And march the streets of Birmingham
To make our country free."

"No, baby, no, you may not go,
For I fear those guns will fire.
But you may go to church instead
And sing in the children's choir."

She has combed and brushed her night-dark hair,
And bathed rose petal sweet,
And drawn white gloves on her small brown hands,
And white shoes on her feet.

The mother smiled to know her child
Was in the sacred place,
But that smile was the last smile
To come upon her face.

For when she heard the explosion,
Her eyes grew wet and wild.
She raced through the streets of Birmingham
Calling for her child.

She clawed through bits of glass and brick,
Then lifted out a shoe.
"O, here's the shoe my baby wore,
But, baby, where are you?"

June Jordan
....

THE TEST OF ATLANTA 1979—

What kind of a person would kill Black children?
What kind of a person could persuade eighteen
different Black children to get into a car or
a truck or a van?
What kind of a person could kill or kidnap
these particular
Black children:

          Edward Hope Smith, 14 years old, dead
          Alfred James Evans, 14 years old, dead
          Yosef Bell, 9 years old, dead
          Milton Harvey, 14 years old, dead
          Angel Lanier, 12 years old, dead
          Eric Middlebrooks, 14 years old, dead
          Christopher Richardson, 11 years old, dead
          Aaron Wyche, 11 years old, dead
          LaTanya Wilson, 7 years old, dead
          Anthony B. Carter, 9 years old, dead
          Earl Lee Terrell, 10 years old, dead
          Clifford Jones, 13 years old, dead
          Aaron Jackson, Jr., 9 years old, dead
          Patrick Rogers, 16 years old, dead
          Charles Stevens, 12 years old, dead
          Jeffrey Lamar Mathis, 10 years old, missing
          Darron Glass, 10 years old, missing
          Lubie "Chuck" Geter, 14 years old, dead

What kind of a person could kill a Black child
and then kill another Black child and then
kill another Black child and then kill another
Black child and then kill another
Black child and then kill another Black
child
and stay above suspicion?
What about the police?
What about somebody Black?
What sixteen year old would say no to a cop?
What seven year old would say no thanks to me?
What is an overreaction to murder?
What kind of a person could kill a Black

child and then kill a Black child and then
kill a Black child?

What kind of a person are you?
What kind of a person am I?

What makes you so sure?

What kind of a person could save a Black child?

What kind of a people will lay down its
life for the lives of our children?

What kind of a people are we?

Ntozake Shange
....

ABOUT ATLANTA

cuz he's black & poor
he's disappeared
the name waz lost   the games werent played
nobody tucks him in at night/ wipes traces
of cornbread & syrup from his fingers
the corners of his mouth
cuz he's black & poor/ he's not
just gone
disappeared one day
& his blood soaks up what's awready red
in atlanta

no ropes this time   no tar & feathers
werent no parades of sheets fires & crosses
nothing/ no signs

....

empty bunkbeds
mothers who forget & cook too much on sundays
just gone/ disappeared
cuz he's black & poor   he's gone
took a bus/ never heard from again

but somebody heard a child screaming
            & went right on ahead
children disappearing/ somewhere in the woods/ decaying
just gone/ disappeared/ in atlanta

mothers are always at the window watching
caint nobody disappear right in fronta yr eyes
but who knows what we cd do
when we're black & poor
we aint here no way/ how cd we disappear?
who wd hear us screaming?

say it was a man with a badge & some candy
say it was a man with a badge & some money
say it was a maniac
cd be more n sticks n stones
gotta be more than stars n stripes
children caint play war when they in one.
caint make believe they dyin/ when they are
caint imagine what they'll be/ cuz they wont
just gone/ disappeared

oh mary dont you weep & dont you moan
oh mary dont you weep & dont you moan
HOLLAR i say HOLLAR
cuz we black & poor & we just disappear

we cant find em   jesus cant find em
til they seepin in soil
father reekin in soil
they bones bout disappeared
they lives aint never been
bleeding where the earth's awready red
dyin cuz they took a bus
& mama caint see that far out her window

the front porch dont go from here to eternity
& they gone
just disappeared

but somebody heard them screaming
somebody crushed them children's bones
somebody's walkin who shd be crawling
for killing who aint never been
cuz we black & poor/ we just be gone

no matter how sweet/ no matter how quiet
just gone
be right back ma
going to the store mother dear
see ya later nana
call ya when i get there mama
& the soil runs red with our dead in atlanta
cuz somebody went right on ahead
crushing them lil bones/ strangling them frail wails
cuz we black & poor
our blood soaks up dirt
while we disappearing

mamas keep looking out the door
saying "i wonder where is my child/ i wonder
           where is my child"
she dont turn the bed back cuz she knows
we black & poor
& we just disappear/ be gone

oh mary dont you weep & dont you moan
oh mary dont you weep & dont you moan
i wonder where is my child
i wonder where is my child

nothing/ no signs
in atlanta

Michael S. Harper

....

ALICE

'The word made stone, the stone word'
'A RITE *is an action the very form of which is the result of a Divine Revelation.'*

I
You stand waist-high in snakes
beating the weeds for the gravebed
a quarter mile from the nearest
relative, an open field in Florida: lost,
looking for Zora, and when she speaks
from her sunken chamber to call
you to her side, she calls
you her distant cousin, her sister
come to mark her burial place
with bright black stone.
She has known you would do this—
her crooked stick, her straight lick—
and the lie you would have to tell
to find her, and that you lied
to her relatives in a conjure-riddle
of the words you have uttered,
calling her to communion.

A black rock of ages you have placed
where there was no marker,
and though the snakes abound
in this preserve from ancestral space,
you have paid your homage

in traditional line, the face open:
your face in the woman-light of surrender
toughened in what you were.

II
Floods of truth flow from your limbs
of these pages in a vision swollen
in experience and pain:
that child you stepped into blossom
of a man's skull beaten into smile
of submission, you gathering horse nectar
for offering over a baby's crusted gasp,
for centuries of motherhood and atonement
for which you write, and the rite written.

And for this I say your name: Alice,
my grandmother's name, your name,
conjured in snake-infested field
where Zora Neale welcomed you home,
and where I speak from now
on higher ground of her risen
black marker where you have written
your name in hers, and in mine.

bell hooks

. . . .

THE BODY INSIDE THE SOUL

i am listening for your footsteps death
i am waiting here
with my young hammer
here with my little knife
i shall pound your fingers
as you open the door
i shall grind them like corn
i shall make bread
i shall sing a praise song
a song my mother taught me
the earth
it is round
there is no edge
there is no way to fall off

bell hooks

. . . .

THE WOMAN'S MOURNING SONG

i cry   comfort
i cry high   the warrior in me returns
this mourning song   to slay sorrow
my heart rises   to make the bread
sun in hand   to sing the mourning song
to make the bread   i cry high
i rise   i cry high
my heavy work hand   i cry
needs   the mourning song
the voice of many singers   go away death
alone   go from love's house
the warmth of many ovens   go make your empty bed

Garth Tate

·········

LAST INSTRUCTIONS

and when i die,
when this old spirit
spurts into God's
unseen air don't shed
one tear,
sisters and brothers instead
rejoice with song and prayer;
paint landscapes of heaven
for the eyes of our children
please don't grieve
my departure, friends
for we shall meet again
in time. . . .

i'll be watching and waiting
your time. . . .

and hand you real freedom
to wrap around your shoulders
like a magic, marvelous cloak

so, when i cross that river,
don't get dressed in dark
colors or collapse before
useless coffins or cry
when you could be wishing
   me well
please don't waste words
on endless oratory
and kill several others
with boredom or dolor
when the sun is still shining golden

just believe that our
span of time is ultimately
god's piece of time and say
that this time
he was a poet and
this time he was black
and next time there's just no
telling how he may come
back.

Quincy Troupe

·········

CONJURING AGAINST ALIEN SPIRITS
for Ishmael Reed

if there is something that takes you
to the brink of terror
turn your pockets inside out, like a lolling dog's
tongue, salivating, in heat, make a screech
owl's death cry go away, go away
make a screech owl's death
cry go away, go away

turn shoes upside down at your own
front door, tie a knot in your apron string, mama
sister, throw fire on salt
talk to raw head & bloody bones
make a hoot owl screaming death
go home, take it away
make a hoot owl take it away, on home

turn your pillowcase inside out
see a cross-eyed, devilish fool. cross
your fingers—drop goobadust in your mind medicine
eat a root doctor's magic root—spit on them, sho-nuff
make a cross in the road
where you met yourself coming
& going, spit on it

that same spot where you passed over
just now, in the road, spit on it, to soften up enemies
walk backwards, along any road you have passed over
before, a red moon, like a one-eyed wino's stare
stuck in bone shadowed trees, there
throw dirt over your left shoulder
spit down on it, in the road
spit down on that same spot
where your terror locked into itself
locked into another enigma
where someone's footprints leave their signatures
of weight, define shapes of worn soles
speak to raw head & bloody bones
great-great-great grandmama
make a hoot owl screaming death

take his case all the way home
screaming, all the way home
make a hoot owl screaming death

take your death slip, all the way home

Ntozake Shange
....

MY FATHER IS A RETIRED MAGICIAN

(for ifa, p.t., & bisa)

my father is a retired magician
which accounts for my irregular behavior
everythin comes outta magic hats
or bottles wit no bottoms & parakeets
are as easy to get as a couple a rabbits
or 3 fifty cent pieces/ 1958

my daddy retired from magic & took
up another trade cuz this friend of mine
from the 3rd grade asked to be made white
on the spot

what cd any self-respectin colored american magician
do wit such a outlandish request/ cept
put all them razzamatazz hocus pocus zippity-do-dah
thingamajigs away   cuz
colored chirren believin in magic
waz becomin politically dangerous for the race
& waznt nobody gonna be made white
on the spot   just
from a clap of my daddy's hands

& the reason i'm so peculiar's
cuz i been studyin up on my daddy's technique
& everythin i do is magic these days
& it's very colored
very now you see it/ now you
dont mess wit me
                        i come from a family of retired
sorcerers/ active houngans & pennyante fortune tellers
wit 41 million spirits critturs & celestial bodies
on our side
                i'll listen to yr problems
                help wit yr career   yr lover   yr wanderin spouse
                make yr grandma's stay in heaven more gratifyin
                ease yr mother thru menopause & show yr son
                how to clean his room

·········

YES YES YES   3 wishes is all you get
                    scarlet ribbons for yr hair
                        benwa balls via hong kong
                            a miniature of machu picchu

all things are possible
but aint no colored magician in her right mind
gonna make you   white
        i mean
                this is blk magic
you lookin at
                & i'm fixin you up good/ fixin you up good n colored
& you gonna be colored all yr life
& you gonna love it/ bein colored/ all yr life/ colored & love it
love it/ bein colored/

SPELL # 7 FROM UPNORTH-OUTWEST GEECHEE JIBARA QUIK MAGIC TRANCE
MANUAL FOR TECHNOLOGICALLY STRESSED THIRD WORLD PEOPLE

RITUALS: MUSIC, DANCE & SPORTS

Ntozake Shange

I LIVE IN MUSIC

i live in music
is this where you live
i live here in music
i live on c# street
my friend lives on b♭ avenue
do you live here in music
sound
falls round me like rain on other folks
saxophones wet my face
cold as winter in st. louis
hot like peppers i rub on my lips
thinkin they waz lilies
i got 15 trumpets where other women got hips
& a upright bass for both sides of my heart
i walk round in a piano like somebody
else/ be walkin on the earth
i live in music
     live in it
        wash in it
i cd even smell it
wear sound on my fingers
sound falls   so fulla music
ya cd make a river where yr arm is &
hold yrself
       hold yrself in a music

Bob Kaufman

....

BATTLE REPORT

One thousand saxophones infiltrate the city,
Each with a man inside,
Hidden in ordinary cases,
Labeled FRAGILE.

A fleet of trumpets drops their hooks,
Inside at the outside.

Ten waves of trombones approach the city
Under blue cover
Of late autumn's neo-classical clouds.

Five hundred bassmen, all string feet tall,
Beating it back to the bass.

One hundred drummers, each a stick in each hand,
The delicate rumble of pianos, moving in.

The secret agent, an innocent bystander,
Drops a note in the wail box.

Five generals, gathered in the gallery,
Blowing plans.

At last, the secret code is flashed:
Now is the time, now is the time.

Attack: The sound of jazz.

The city falls.

Amina Baraka

....

ALL IS ONE FOR MONK

caught me sittin
on a stoop in the 50s
in love w/dark glasses
& berets
off chords, & split notes
black stockings
& no bra
breakin Free
me make-up
straight,
chasin Monk
to watch the piano player
dance
slides, runs, turns &
quick steps
over-there/some-where
arms holdin up the sound
"Off Minor"
tunes riffin
"Jackie-ing"
Sets w/Monk
dealin
& you
you couldn't be there
if you couldn't Be-Bop

DEAR JOHN, DEAR COLTRANE

a love supreme, a love supreme
a love supreme, a love supreme

Sex fingers toes
in the marketplace
near your father's church
in Hamlet, North Carolina—
witness to this love
in this calm fallow
of these minds,
there is no substitute for pain:
genitals gone or going,
seed burned out,
you tuck the roots in the earth,
turn back, and move
by river through the swamps,
singing: *a love supreme, a love*
supreme;
what does it all mean?
Loss, so great each black
woman expects your failure
in mute change, the seed gone.
You plod up into the electric city—
your song now crystal and
the blues. You pick up the horn
with some will and blow
into the freezing night:
a love supreme, a love supreme—

Dawn comes and you cook
up the thick sin 'tween
impotence and death, fuel

the tenor sax cannibal
heart, genitals and sweat
that makes you clean—
a love supreme, a love supreme—

Why you so black?
cause I am
why you so funky?
cause I am
why you so black?
cause I am
why you so sweet?
cause I am
why you so black?
cause I am
a love supreme, a love supreme:

So sick
you couldn't play *Naima,*
so flat we ached
for song you'd concealed
with your own blood,
your diseased liver gave
out its purity,
the inflated heart
pumps out, the tenor kiss,
tenor love:
a love supreme, a love supreme—
a love supreme, a love supreme—

Larry Neal

....

DON'T SAY GOODBYE TO THE PORK-PIE HAT

(For Langston Hughes)

Don't say goodbye to the pork-pie hat that rolled along on padded shoulders,
                  that swang be-bop phrases
                  in Minton's jelly-roll dreams.
don't say goodbye to hip hats tilted in the style of a soulful era,
the pork-pie hat that Lester dug,
swirling in the sound of sun saxes,
repeating phrase on phrase, repeating bluely
as hi-hat cymbals crash and trumpets scream while
musicians move in and out of this gloom; the pork-pie hat reigns supreme,
the elegance of style
gleaned from the city's underbelly.
                  tonal memories
                  tonal memories
of salt-peanuts and hot house birds. the pork-pie hat
                                    sees.
And who was the musician who
              blew Bird way by accident, then died, obscure,
an obscene riff repeating lynch scenes?
repeating weird changes. The chorus repeats itself also, the horns slide
from note to note in blue, in blue streaks of mad wisdom;
blues notes
coiling around
the pork-pie hat and the drum-dancing hips defying the sanctity of white
America.

and who was the trumpet player in that small town in Kansas who
  begged to sit in,
blew a chorus, then fainted dead on the bandstand?
blew you away.
that same musician resurrected himself in Philly at the Blue Note Cafe
    Ridge Avenue and 16th St.
after the third set, had him an old horn and was wearing the pork-pie
    hat.
wasn't he familiar? didn't you think that you were seeing a ghost?
and didn't the pork-pie hat leave Minton's
    for 52nd St.?
and didn't it later make it to Paris where they dug him too?
and didn't the pork-pie buy Bird a meal in '35
when said musician was kicked out of the High-Hat (18th & South)
      for blowing
strange changes?

I saw the pork-pie hat skimming the horizon
    flashing bluegreenyellowlights
he was blowing black stars
and
weird looneymoon changes and chords were wrapped around him
      and he was flying
fast, zipping past note, past sound into cosmic silence.
Caresses flowed from the voice in the horn in the blue
of the yellow whiskey room where hustlers
with big coats and fly sisters moved; finger popping while
    tearing at chicken and waffles—
the pork-pie hat loomed specter like, a vision for the world,
dressed in a camel hair coat, shiny knob toe shoes, sporting
a hip pin stripe suit with pants pressed razor sharp, caressing his horn
    baby-like.

And who was the bitch in the bar in Boston who kept trying to make it
with the pork-pie hat while it fingered for the changes
on Dewey Square? She almost make you blow your cool.
you did blow your cool, 'cause on the side I got you hollered
shut-up across that slick white boy's
tape recorder. Yeah the one who copped your music & made
some fat money after you died. didn't you
                              blow your cool?
and didn't you almost lose your pork-pie hat behind all that shit?
Who was the ofay chick that followed the group
                              from Boston to Philly
                              from New York to Washington
                              from Chicago to Kansas City
                              was that Backstage Sally?
or was Backstage Sally a blue-voiced soul sister who lived
                                        on Brown street in Philly.
who dug you, who fed you cold nights with soul food
and soul-body. was that Backstage Sally?
Sounds drift above the cities of Black America;
all over America black musicians are putting
on the pork-pie hat again, picking up their axes,
preparing to blow away the white dream. you can
hear them screeching love in rolling sheets of sound;
with movement and rhythm recreating themselves and the world;
sounds splintering the deepest regions of the spiritual universe—
crisp and moaning voices leaping in the horns of destruction,
blowing doom and death to all who have no use for the Spirit.
don't say goodbye to the pork-pie hat, it lives. Yeah . . .

Lester lives and leaps
Delancey's dilemma is over
Bird lives
Lady lives
Eric stands next to me
while I finger the afro-horn
Bird lives
Lady lives
Lester leaps in every night
Tad's delight
is mine now
Dinah knows
Fats and Wardell blow fours
Dinah knows
Richie knows
that Bud is Buddha
that Bird is Shango
that Jelly Roll dug ju-ju
and Lester lives
in Ornette's leaping
the blues live
we live. live
spirit lives. the sound
lives bluebirdlives
lives and leaps. dig
the bluevoices
dig the pork pie dig
the spirit in Sun Ra's sound. dig
spirit lives in sound
lives sound spirit
sound lives in spirit
spirit lives in sound. blow.
spirit lives
spirit lives
spirit lives
SPIRIT . . . . . !!!! . . . . . SWHEEEEEET !!!!
   Take it
      again, this time from the chorus

HOW LONG HAS TRANE BEEN GONE

Tell me about the good things
you clappin & laughin

Will you remember
or will you forget

Forget about the good things
like Blues & Jazz being black
Yeah Black Music
all about you

And the musicians that
write & play about you
a Black brother groanin
a Black sister moanin
& beautiful Black children
ragged. . underfed laughin
not knowin

Will you remember their names
or do they have no names
no lives—only products
to be used when you wanna
dance fuck & cry

You takin—they givin
You livin—they
creating starving dying
trying to make a better tomorrow
Giving you & your children a history
But what do you care about
history—Black History
and John Coltrane
No
All you wanna do
is pat your foot
sip a drink & pretend
with your head bobbin up & down

What do you care about acoustics
bad microphones or out-of-tune pianos
& noise
You the club owners & disc jockeys
made a deal didn't you
a deal about Black Music
& you really don't give
a shit long as you take

There was a time
when certain radio stations played all Black Music
from Charlie Parker to Johnny Ace
on show after show
but what happened
I'll tell you what happened
they divided Black Music
doubled the money
& left us split again
is what happened

John Coltranes dead & some
of you
have yet to hear him play
How long how long has that Trane been gone

and how many more Tranes will go
before you understand your life
John Coltrane who had the whole of
life wrapped up in B flat
John Coltrane like Malcolm
True image of Black Masculinity

Now tell me about the good things
I'm telling you about
John Coltrane

A name that should ring
throughout the projects mothers

Mothers with sons
who need John Coltrane
Need the warm arm of his music
like words from a Father
words of Comfort
words of Africa
words of Welcome
How long how long has that Trane been gone

John palpitating love notes
in a lost-found nation
within a nation
His music resounding discovery
signed Always
John Coltrane

Rip those dead white people off
your walls Black People
Black People whose walls
should be a hall
A Black Hall Of Fame
so our children will know
will know & be proud
Proud to say I'm from Parker City—Coltrane City—Ornette City
Pharoah City living on Holiday Street next to
James Brown park in the State of Malcolm

How Long
how long
will it take for you to understand
that Tranes been gone
riding in a portable radio
next to your son who's lonely
Who walks walks walks into nothing
no city no state no home no nothing
how long
How long
Have Black People been gone

George Barlow

MINGUS SPEAKS: FOUND POEMS

1.
the soloists
at Birdland

had to wait for
Parker's next record

to find out
what to play

   what
will they do now

2.
   hey dig
Bird ain't dead
he's hiding out
somewhere

& he'll be back
with some new shit

that will scare
everyone to death

for Bird

Sterling A. Brown

MA RAINEY

I

When Ma Rainey
Comes to town,
Folks from anyplace
Miles aroun',
From Cape Girardeau,
Poplar Bluff,
Flocks in to hear
Ma do her stuff;
Comes flivverin' in,
Or ridin' mules,
Or packed in trains,
Picknickin' fools. . . .
That's what it's like,
Fo' miles on down,
To New Orleans delta
An' Mobile town,
When Ma hits
Anywheres aroun'.

II

Dey comes to hear Ma Rainey from de little river settlements,
From blackbottom cornrows and from lumber camps;
Dey stumble in de hall, jes a-laughin' an' a-cacklin',
Cheerin' lak roarin' water, lak wind in river swamps.

An' some jokers keeps deir laughs a-goin' in de crowded aisles,
An' some folks sits dere waitin' wid deir aches an' miseries,
Till Ma comes out before dem, a-smilin' gold-toofed smiles
An' Long Boy ripples minors on de black an' yellow keys.

III

O Ma Rainey,
Sing yo' song;
Now you's back
Whah you belong,
Git way inside us,
Keep us strong. . . .

O Ma Rainey,
Li'l an' low;
Sing us 'bout de hard luck
Roun' our do';
Sing us 'bout de lonesome road
We mus' go. . . .

IV
I talked to a fellow, an' the fellow say,
"She jes' catch hold of us, somekindaway.
She sang Backwater Blues one day:

    'It rained fo' days an' de skies was dark as night,
    Trouble taken place in de lowlands at night.

    'Thundered an' lightened an' the storm begin to roll
    Thousan's of people ain't got no place to go.

    'Den I went an' stood upon some high ol' lonesome hill,
    An' looked down on the place where I used to live.'

An' den de folks, dey natchally bowed dey heads an' cried,
Bowed dey heavy heads, shet dey moufs up tight an' cried,
An' Ma lef' de stage, an' followed some de folks outside."

Dere wasn't much more de fellow say:
She jes' gits hold of us dataway.

Jayne Cortez
....

SO MANY FEATHERS

You danced a magnetic dance
in your rhinestones and satin banana G-strings
it was you who cut the river
with your pink diamond tongue
did the limbo on your back
straight from the history of southern flames
onto the stage where your body
covered in metallic flint
under black and green feathers strutted
with wings of a vulture paradise on your head
strutted among the birds
until you became terror woman of all feathers
of such terrible beauty
of such fire
such flames
all feathers Josephine
This Josephine
exploding red marble eyes in new york
this Josephine
breaking color bars in miami
this Josephine
mother of orphans
legion of honor
rosette of resistance
this Josephine before
splitting the solidarity of her beautiful feathers

Feather-woman of terror
such feathers so beautiful
Josephine
with your frosted mouth half-open
why split your flamingos
with the death white boers in durban south africa
Woman with magnificent face of Ife mask
why all the teeth for the death white boers in durban
Josephine you had every eyelash in the forest
every feather flying
why give your beaded snake-hips
to the death white boers in durban

Josephine didn't you know about the torture
chambers
made of black flesh and feathers
made by the death white boers in durban
Josephine terror-woman of terrible beauty of such
feathers
I want to understand why dance
the dance of the honorary white
for the death white boers in durban

After all Josephine
I saw you in your turquoise headdress
with royal blue sequins pasted on your lips
your fantastic legs studded with emeralds
as you kicked   as you bumped   as you leaped in the
air
then froze
your body breaking lightning in fish net
and Josephine   Josephine
what a night in harlem
what electricity
such trembling
such goose pimples
so many feathers
Josephine
dancer of the magnetic dancers
of the orange flint pelvis of the ruby navel
of the purple throat
of the feet pointing both ways
of feathers now gone
Josephine Josephine
I remember you rosette of resistance
southern flames
Josephine of the birdheads, ostrich plumes
bananas and sparkling G-strings
Josephine of the double-jointed knees
double-jointed shoulders   double-jointed thighs
double-jointed breasts   double-jointed fingers
double-jointed toes   double-jointed eyeballs

double-jointed hips doubling
into a double squat like a double star into a giant
double snake
with the double heartbeats of a young girl
doubling into woman-hood
and grinding into an emulsified double spirit
Josephine terror-woman of feathers   i remember
Josephine of such conflicts   i remember
Josephine of such floating   i remember
Josephine of such heights   i remember
Josephine
of so many transformations   i remember
Josephine
of such beauty   i remember
Josephine of such fire   i remember
Josephine of such sheen   i remember
Josephine
so many feathers   i remember
Josephine   Josephine

Peter Harris
....

SOME SONGS WOMEN SING

(in homage to "If I Were Your Woman" & "Make Me the Woman (You Come Home To)," by Gladys Knight & The Pips; "My Guy," by Mary Wells; "Don't Mess With Bill," by the Marvelettes; "Jimmy Mack," by Martha and The Vandellas; "I Got Him Back in My Arms Again," by The Supremes; "Natural Woman," by Aretha Franklin; "Alfie" & "Message to Michael," by Dionne Warwick; "Yes I'm Ready," by Barbara Mason; "BABY," by Carla Thomas, & other womansung classics . . .)

some songs by women
so bad even men
sing along without changing words
we don't flinch
promising to keep
some wayward brother
"weak as a lamb"
we confess "there's not a man today
can tear me away from My Guy"
we be warning all the sisters
"Don't Mess With Bill"
begging Jimmy Mack
"when are you comin' back?"
announce with pride
"I got him back in my arms again"
One Voice sings these songs
no tittering come time
to sing some man back home
no stuttering come time
to moan he makes me real feel
verse by verse
we holler all the words
just as proud to lipsync
Aretha, Gladys, Tammi Terrell
just as satisfied
being Diana, Martha, Bernice Reagon
as ripping into a
Mad Lad/Impression/Stylistic type thing
anyway
what is a Vandella

a Vandella as in
Martha and the . . .
what is a Vandella
anyway
but a call to Imagination
        to rework our minds
        to remember the Each Other
        in each other
        to believe in the Vandella
in all of us
a Vandella
like one of them
Blackcity names
sisters create to sound French
Fashwan LeJean
Que Sera Que Sera
names like Sweet
names like no other
names for all to call
with wonderful wonder
whatever will be
        will be
        will be sung together whether
woman or man sings
long as it touches
the Deep Human
so when Aretha say
        "I didn't know
        just what was
        wrong with me

till your kiss
helped me name it"
I don't even *want*
to be a Natural Man
& I wouldn't never be alone
if I could beg a brother
like Jennifer Holliday
onstage/spotlit/sweatswept
sometimes
one of these womensung classics
rise out radios tearing down walls of gender

from under bricks & cinder
our voices float on time/on tune
to the charming neon leadlady singers
who make us understand
just what it mean
to be a memorable Main Squeeze
just what it mean
to be a Marvelous Marvelette
just what it mean
to believe whatever we'll be
we'll be

Michael S. Harper

....

ALONE

A friend told me
He'd risen above jazz.
I leave him there.

for Miles Davis

Tim Seibles

....

WHO

(for the Lewitsky Dance Co.)

Who doesn't
want to dance
to be inside the body
not somewhere beside it
to feel the arms and legs
hot and clean in a clear lake of air
like fins, as though every limb
were a fish for a moment
free of the water out of the world—
the body, strange as a planet
reeling in its own soft sparkle

Who doesn't want to dance
to let the body go gracefully mad
to fall into the music as though
from a cliff—every muscle a feather
every three feathers a bird every bird
bald blind and falling

as though the fall itself were the dance
as if the music were a cushion of air
a wind holding you up as though
in motion the body is a leaf is a
new fabric better than feathers better than water

Who doesn't want to remember the feet
to wash them in music
to feel gravity's tireless kiss
bringing you back, pulling you in
as if there were only you and the earth
and music were the sea
and the body were a small ship with lungs
as its sails—as though breathing
were dancing and dancing were living
and living were enough. Who
doesn't want to dance?

Eugene B. Redmond

DANCE BODIES #1

Spitfire! from *BlackFleshMotors*
      /whirhums/
Under acrobatic howls:
Zig-grip! Zig-grip! Zig-grip!
Zag-lore! and bodies brush air;
Dip-twist! Down-bend! Dip-twist!
And kissing palms pancake/applaud air,
Chop smoke/humpsreams:
JamesBrowning the breakdown!
BrakeDowning the JamesBrown!
Washing air with sugarsweat/
With antiseptic potion and polish;
Caroling *fleshmotors* flinging/
Ringing from shirt or skirt:
        "Boogaloo on through!
        Breakdown the walls, brother!
        Boogaloo on through!"
Footfire on floor of hot coals:
Split! Get up! Toe turn!
        /Split!/ /Toe-turn!/
Heel-tunes screeching:
        "Bank-here! Break-there!"
Kissing palms pancake/paralyze the air:
Sugarsweat sterilizing air
With gymnastic intelligence/
With braindance acrobatics/
With spitfire from *fleshmotors*—humming:
        "Boogaloo on through!
        Breakdown the walls, brother!
        Boogaloo on through!"

Jayne Cortez
·········

TAPPING

(for Baby Laurence, and other tap dancers)

When i pat this floor
  with my tap

when i slide on air
  and fill this horn intimate with
the rhythm of my two drums

   when i cross   kick
scissor   locomotive

   take four for nothing
four we're gone

when the solidarity of my yoruba turns
join these vibrato feet
  in a Johnny Hodges lick
a chorus of insistent Charlie Parker riffs

   when i stretch out for a chromatic split
together with my double X
   converging in a quartet of circles

when i dance my spine in a slouch
  slur my lyrics with a heel slide
arch these insteps in free time

  when i drop my knees
when i fold my hands
  when i decorate this atmosphere
with a Lester Young leap and
  enclose my hip like snake repetitions
in a chanting proverb
  of the freeze

I'm gonna spotlite my boogie
  in a Coltrane yelp

echo my push in a Coleman Hawkins whine

i'm gonna frog my hunch in a Duke Ellington
  strut

quarter stroke my rattle
  like an Albert Ayler cry

i'm gonna accent my march in a Satchmo pitch

  triple my grind in a Ma Rainey blues

i'm gonna steal no steps

  i'm gonna pay my dues

i'm gonna 1 2 3

  and let the people in the apple
go hmmmp hmmmmp hmmmmmp

A. B. Spellman
....
THE TWIST

a dancer's world
is walls, movement
confined: music:

god's last breath.
rhythm: the last beating
of his heart. a dancer

follows that sound, blind
to its source, toward walls, with
others, she cannot dance alone.

she thinks of thought as
windows, as ice around the dance.
can you break it? move.

Harryette Mullen
....
THE DANCE SHE DOES
for Judith Jamison

Judith dances on my wall.
She's barefoot on the bare floor.
She's a long shadow in the yellow
squares
of three tall sunlight windows.
Her eloquent body speaking
in an empty room.

That room in which she dances
is my church.
Those sunshafts through the windows
are my hymns of joy.
The dance she does
is my religion.

Her body,
the Sunday sermon.

OUT OF THE WAILING

I Hold A Lust To See People
See them moving,
Waltzing and bopping

Moving and Doing Things
Natural to their Souls

Like Singing Opera
Like Dancing Ballet
Like Playing Joplin

Waltzing, Bopping
Doing the Rag

Naturally to their Souls

Moving and Doing Things
Uplifting and Renewing

Like Blooming and Becoming

Like Popping Blues
Like Hopping Reggae
Like Shouting Spirituals
Like Humming Hymns
Like Clicking Tap . . .

I Hold A Lust To See People
To See My People
In Holy Orchestration:

From Pyramids
To Skyscrapers

From cutting celery
To Sweeping Floors

From Office Windows
To Factory Doors

From Mango Groves
To Shipping decks

From Stylish Mansions
To Shotgun Houses

I Hold A Lust To See My People

See Them Moving
Moving and Doing

Doing Things Natural

Like Surviving—
High-Stepping Style,
With Souls Intact

Like Looking
In The Mirror
And Smiling Back.

Natasha Tarpley

....

FEEL FREE

The year the white women came like the plague
was when me and my girls took to backwater
cornfields and the shimmy
girl I love the way you shake
Time lunch bell rang, we was out at Roderick's field
barefoot and loose headed
Marva pounded a beat on her thigh and Frieda
stepped
    stepped
like walking to Jesus
do the snake girl
and wound herself up to trembling
We would come in then, hard and fast,
shaking till sweat dripped from our fingers
Marva stopped her beat, but we would still be going on
the sound of our own feet, the screaming of crows,
the wind slapping cornstalks,
even a heartbeat
Some say we was begging for the devil
But we was just dancing
And when we got through, that field vibrated,
like all of Memphis rolling beneath us
In the place where Frieda stood,
the ground was worn to the roots
Even the earth could not resist that
step
We was bad bad girls

Cornelius Eady

....

MY MOTHER,
IF SHE HAD WON FREE DANCE LESSONS

Would she have been a person
With a completely different outlook on life?
There are times when I visit
And find her settled on a chair
In our dilapidated house,
The neighborhood crazy lady
Doing what the neighborhood crazy lady is
    supposed to do,
Which is absolutely nothing

And I wonder as we talk our sympathetic talk,
Abandoned in easy dialogue,
I, the son of the crazy lady,
Who crosses easily into her point of view
As if yawning
Or taking off an overcoat.
Each time I visit
I walk back into our lives

And I wonder, like any child who wakes up one day
    to find themself
Abandoned in a world larger than their
    Bad dreams,
I wonder as I see my mother sitting there,
Landed to the right-hand window in the living room,
Pausing from time to time in the endless loop
    of our dialogue
To peek for rascals through the
Venetian blinds,

I wonder a small thought.
I walk back into our lives.
Given the opportunity,
How would she have danced?
Would it have been as easily
As we talk to each other now,
The crazy lady
And the crazy lady's son,

As if we were old friends from opposite coasts
Picking up the thread of a long conversation,

Or two ballroom dancers
Who only know
One step?

What would have changed
If the phone had rung like a suitor,
If the invitation had arrived in the mail
Like Jesus, extending a hand?

Claude McKay
....

THE HARLEM DANCER

Applauding youths laughed with young prostitutes
And watched her perfect, half-clothed body sway;
Her voice was like the sound of blended flutes
Blown by black players upon a picnic day.
She sang and danced on gracefully and calm,
The light gauze hanging loose about her form;
To me she seemed a proudly-swaying palm
Grown lovelier for passing through a storm.
Upon her swarthy neck black shiny curls
Luxuriant fell; and tossing coins in praise,
The wine-flushed, bold-eyed boys, and even the girls,
Devoured her shape with eager, passionate gaze;
But looking at her falsely-smiling face,
I knew her self was not in that strange place.

Al Young

A DANCE FOR MA RAINEY

I'm going to be just like you, Ma
Rainey this monday morning
clouds puffing up out of my head
like those balloons
that float above the faces of white people
in the funnypapers

I'm going to hover in the corners
of the world, Ma
& sing from the bottom of hell
up to the tops of high heaven
& send out scratchless waves of yellow
& brown & that basic black honey
misery

I'm going to cry so sweet
& so low
& so dangerous,
Ma,
that the message is going to reach you
back in 1922
where you shimmer
snaggle-toothed
perfumed &
powdered
in your bauble beads

hair pressed & tied back
throbbing with that sick pain
I know
& hide so well
that pain that blues
jives the world with
aching to be heard
that downness
that bottomlessness
first felt by some stolen delta nigger
swamped under with redblooded american
agony;
reduced to the sheer shit
of existence
that bred
& battered us all,
Ma,
the beautiful people
our beautiful people
our beautiful brave black people
who no longer need to jazz
or sing to themselves in murderous vibrations
or play the veins of their strong tender arms
with needles
to prove how proud we are

Ishmael Reed

....

THE BLACK COCK

for Jim Hendrix, HooDoo from his natural born

He frightens all the witches and the dragons in their lair
He cues the clear blue daylight and He gives the night its dare
He flaps His wings for warning and He struts atop a mare
for when He crows they quiver and when He comes they flee

In His coal black plumage and His bright red crown
and His golden beaked fury and His calculated frown
in His webbed footed glory He sends Jehovah down
for when He crows they quiver and when He comes they flee

O they dance around the fire and they boil the gall of wolves
and they sing their strange crude melodies and play their
weirder tunes and the villagers close their windows and the grave-
yard starts to heave and the cross wont help their victims and
the screaming fills the night and the young girls die with
open eyes and the skies are lavender light
but when He crows they quiver and when He comes they flee

Well the sheriff is getting desperate as they go their nature's way
killing cattle smothering infants slaughtering those who block their way
and the countryside swarms with numbness as their magic circle grows
but when He crows they tremble and when He comes they flee

Posting hex-signs on their wagons simple worried farmers pray
passing laws and faking justice only feed the witches brew
violet stones are rendered helpless drunken priests are helpless too
but when He crows they quiver and when He comes they flee

We have seen them in their ritual we have catalogued their crimes
we are weary of their torture but we cannot bring them down
their ancient hoodoo enemy who does the work, the trick,
strikes peril in their dead fiend's hearts and pecks their flesh to quick
love Him feed Him He will never let you down
for when He crows they quiver and when He comes they frown

....

ZOOM (THE COMMODORES)

i once drove to Atlantic City
in the middle of the night
i crept thru a thunderstorm
for the Spinners/Harold Melvin & the Bluenotes
& motherfathersisterbrother
otherwise known as MFSB
i lost my voice for love
ever since doo-wap i've been weak
for the sound of Philadelphia
it's well known
i remember the Howard/ the Apollo
a few roadhouses
& even Ester's Orbit Room
sweaty funky overweight underbuilt joints
where you could buy to satisfy
any of your senses
where romance flourished in the garish pink lights
and sweet night of the Coasters/ the Tempts
& sweet Smokey's Miracles
oh! where romance had a chance/was the chance
the only chance any of us had
young college students don't like to discuss it
young poets eschew it
but after the Club Harlem & sandy crab cakes
under conk lights & dawn drunks
across the street i found the Commodores
known for the profound rhymes of our times
like "it's slippery when it's wet"
the tasteless fleshiness of the seventies
can be redeemed if you just learn to "Zoom"
"Zoom" saves love & rescues romance
"Zoom" "i'd like to take just a moment
& dream my dreams"
zoom you Commodores
with all the footlight ardor & corn
with all the foolish sincerity of a man
who don't care who knows/bout his jones
his love/his woman/his sweet thing
his squeeze/his weakness

his nose that a truck could run up
his crush/his sun/his moon/his starship
the sunshine of his life/ the apple of his eye
his queen/ his dream/ his ZOOM
you can tell me all that/ i don't mind
zoom i'm with you Commodores
talking trash is one of the lost arts
of making love & giving humanity a break
zoom i'm with you Commodores
cause you meant it/ and you loved her
and you did fly to that good woman
who waited/ who waited for her baby
her man/ her jones/her sweet daddy
her good thing/ her love/her only one
her sun/ her moon/ sweet nights in june
her honey/her sweetheart
her ship that was comin in/ her Zoom
you Commodores
maybe you are the best of us
that can love & believe
all our foolish triteness
& the way we can't talk when it's important
& the love that can keep death waiting
til we see those eyes one more time
zoom i love you Commodores
i wann fly away from here too
zoom i love you
when you call in the night
cause you couldn't catch a cab
cause you see things in the dark
zoom i love you when you use subterfuge
to get me alone/when you drop hints/or drop by
when you promise me everything cause i'm so divine
zoom i love you
cause you won't say no/cause you don't want to go
cause it's so cruel without love
give me the tacky grandeur of Atlantic City
on the fourth of july
the corny promises of Motown
give me the romance & the Zoom

Lenard D. Moore

·········

A BLUESMAN'S BLUES

What is not rooted in static
should soothe the ear:
a bluesman's blues
flaring the air as he fires
notes so exact
they rise, tonal as wind, as swift;
his voice spreads a chill,
skybound, through thinnest air
at the moment of silence
withdraws itself, within itself
as blue duskfall
slows to a deeper essence
and turns inward into the dark.

The thin blues man glisters.
Sweat trembles on his lips
in his too-hot story
when blues notes appear unforced
into a night of song.

How clear this autumn night:
the songman wearing leather
and turning away from his shadow,
while a voice so unlike itself,
repeats itself
like wind on raw air.
And our ears are sound
tuning into themselves
against the moon's white rising.

THE WEARY BLUES

Droning a drowsy syncopated tune,
Rocking back and forth to a mellow croon,
    I heard a Negro play.
Down on Lenox Avenue the other night
By the pale dull pallor of an old gas light
    He did a lazy sway. . . .
    He did a lazy sway. . . .
To the tune o' those Weary Blues.
With his ebony hands on each ivory key
He made that poor piano moan with melody.
    O Blues!
Swaying to and fro on his rickety stool
He played that sad raggy tune like a musical fool.
    Sweet Blues!
Coming from a black man's soul.
    O Blues!
In a deep song voice with a melancholy tone
I heard that Negro sing, that old piano moan—
    "Ain't got nobody in all this world,
    Ain't got nobody but ma self.
    I's gwine to quit ma frownin'
    And put ma troubles on the shelf."
Thump, thump, thump, went his foot on the floor.
He played a few chords then he sang some more—
    "I got the Weary Blues
    And I can't be satisfied.
    Got the Weary Blues
    And can't be satisfied—
    I ain't happy no mo'
    And I wish that I had died."
And far into the night he crooned that tune.
The stars went out and so did the moon.
The singer stopped playing and went to bed
While the Weary Blues echoed through his head.
He slept like a rock or a man that's dead.

Yusef Komunyakaa

SLAM, DUNK, & HOOK

Fast breaks. Lay ups. With Mercury's
Insignia on our sneakers,
We outmaneuvered the footwork
Of bad angels. Nothing but a hot
Swish of strings like silk
Ten feet out. In the roundhouse
Labyrinth our bodies
Created, we could almost
Last forever, poised in midair
Like storybook sea monsters.
A high note hung there
A long second. Off
The rim. We'd corkscrew
Up & dunk balls that exploded
The skullcap of hope & good
Intention. Bug-eyed, lanky,
All hands & feet . . . sprung rhythm.
We were metaphysical when girls
Cheered on the sidelines.
Tangled up in a falling,

Muscles were a bright motor
Double-flashing to the metal hoop
Nailed to our oak.
When Sonny Boy's mama died
He played nonstop all day, so hard
Our backboard splintered.
Glistening with sweat, we jibed
& rolled the ball off our
Fingertips. Trouble
Was there slapping a blackjack
Against an open palm.
Dribble, drive to the inside, feint,
& glide like a sparrowhawk.
Lay ups. Fast breaks.
We had moves we didn't know
We had. Our bodies spun
On swivels of bone & faith,
Through a lyric slipknot
Of joy, & we knew we were
Beautiful & dangerous.

Michael S. Harper

MAKIN' JUMP SHOTS

He waltzes into the lane
'cross the free-throw line,
fakes a drive, pivots,
floats from the asphalt turf
in an arc of black light,
and sinks two into the chains.

One on one he fakes
down the main, passes
into the free lane
and hits the chains.

A sniff in the fallen air—
he stuffs it through the chains
riding high:
"traveling" someone calls—
and he laughs, stepping
to a silent beat, gliding
as he sinks two into the chains.

Quincy Troupe
....

A POEM FOR "MAGIC"

for Earvin "Magic" Johnson, Donnell Reid & Richard Franklin

take it to the hoop, "magic" johnson
take the ball dazzling down the open lane
herk & jerk & raise your six feet nine inch
frame into air sweating screams of your neon name
"magic" johnson, nicknamed "windex" way back in high school
cause you wiped glass backboards so clean
where you first juked & shook
wiled your way to glory
a new style fusion of shake & bake energy
using everything possible, you created your own space
to fly through — any moment now, we expect your wings
to spread feathers for that spooky take off of yours —
then shake & glide, till you hammer home
a clotheslining deuce off glass
now, come back down with a reverse hoodoo gem
off the spin, & stick it in sweet, popping nets, clean
from twenty feet, right-side

put the ball on the floor, "magic"
slide the dribble behind your back, ease it deftly
between your bony, stork legs, head bobbing everwhichaway
up & down, you see everything on the court
off the high, yoyo patter, stop & go dribble, you shoot
a threading needle rope pass, sweet home to kareem
cutting through the lane, his skyhook pops cords
now lead the fastbreak, hit worthy on the fly
now, blindside a behind the back pinpointpass for two more
off the fake, looking the other way
you raise off balance into space
sweating chants of your name, turn, 180 degrees
off the move, your legs scissoring space, like a swimmer's
yoyoing motion, in deep water, stretching out now toward free
flight, you double pump through human trees, hang in place
slip the ball into your left hand
then deal it like a las vegas card dealer
off squared glass, into nets, living up to your singular nickname
so "bad", you cartwheel the crowd towards frenzy
wearing now your electric smile, neon as your name

in victory, we suddenly sense your glorious uplift
your urgent need to be champion
& so we cheer, rejoicing with you, for this quicksilver, quicksilver
                                                quicksilver
moment of fame, so put the ball on the floor again, "magic"
juke & dazzle, shake & bake down the lane
take the sucker to the hoop, "magic" johnson,
recreate reverse hoodoo gems off the spin,
deal alley-oop-dunk-a-thon-magician passes
now, double-pump, scissor, vamp through space
hang in place & put it all up in the sucker's face, "magic"
johnson, & deal the roundball, like the juju man that you am
like the sho-nuff shaman man that you am
"magic", like the sho-nuff spaceman, you am

George Mosby, Jr.
....

TO JOSH GIBSON (LEGENDARY SLUGGER OF THE OLD NEGRO BASEBALL LEAGUE)

black knight
with thor's hammer in your bat
i've heard how you blasted the hell out of bullets
from the rifle satch and the likes

if grandpa still breathed
he'd swear that the blood in his flesh should freeze
if he were lying
saying "old josh
        now that was the biggest damn bat
        that ever lived"
smiling all the while
in his profession

he'd swear
that even when the babe reigned
he sat on the throne
200 homers (and some) a smaller king
than you
black knight
with thor's hammer in your bat

and it's testimony
that grandpa's tongue was pure
like the serenade
of a wooded stream

Tom Dent
....
FOR COOL PAPA BELL

Hey Cool Papa
I see picture of you in your later
years
tall black skin withered
straight
proud
you must have been a streak of black gold
flashing around the bases like some
great African warrior misplaced . . .
it is said you scored from first on a bunt
against the all-white major league all-stars
you were forty summers then
and they wanted to know how you did it
was it magic
was it voodoo
was it a freak of segregation
was it special compensation for
                        national mental inferiority
                        in the labs of Stanford?
was it something that only happens in colored ball
                        a Saturday night mutation gone insane
                        in the white man's game?

you must have been the genius black musician
of Daho/Sippi carving his own instrument
so now at seventy
they parade you out from
your job as janitor St. Louis
City Hall
and place you in the retroactive
Hall of Fame . . .

and forgive us if we don't cry
Cool Papa
forgive us if we don't get excited
for with you we share the night
of that memory those memories
all the bitter years and buried triumphs
because you did it man
and no one can take away
bitter years
buried triumphs.

Samuel Allen (Paul Vesey)
....
TO SATCH

Sometimes I feel I will *never* stop
Just go on forever
Till one fine mornin
I'm gonna reach up and grab me a handfulla stars
Swing out my long lean leg
And whip three hot strikes burnin down the heavens
And look over at God and say
How about that!

Ishmael Reed

....

WHITE HOPE
for shane stevens

jack johnson licked
one pug so, d man
retired to a farm.
never again opened
his mouth save to
talk abt peachtrees
sow & last year's
almanac;

and whenever somebody
say jack johnson,

he'd get that far away
look.

Yusef Komunyakaa

·········

BOXING DAY

"Burns never landed a blow.
It was hopeless, preposterous,
heroic."—Jack London

This is the spot where Jack Johnson
cornered Tommy Burns in 1908.
Strong as an ironbark
tree, he stood there
flexing his biceps
till he freed himself of kindness
& released the prisoner under his skin.
  The bell clanged
  & a profusion of voices
  shook the afternoon. Johnson
  jabbed with the power
  of an engine throwing a rod,
  & Burns sleepwalked
  to the spinning edge
of the planet like a moth
drawn to a burning candle.
He was dizzy as a drunken girl
tangoing with a flame tree
breaking into full bloom,
burdened by fruits of desire
& the smell of carnival.
  A currawong crossed the sun
  singing an old woman's cry.
  The referee threw in his towel
  in the fourteenth round & bookies

scribbled numbers beside names
  madly, as twenty thousand rose
  into the air like a wave.
For years the razor-gang boys
bragged about how they would've KOed
Johnson, dancing & punching each day.
Eighty years later, the stadium
is checkered with tennis courts,
with a plantation of pale suits
called White City.
  I hear Miles Davis' trumpet
  & Leadbelly's "Titanic."
  A bell's metal treble
  reverberates . . . the sunset
  moves like a tremble of muscle
  across Rushcutters Bay,
  back to the name Johnson
flashing over the teletype
when he danced The Eagle Rock
& drove fast cars & had a woman
on each arm, to Jesse Willard
pushing him down into a whirlpool's
death roll under scintillant
confetti & wild cheers in Havana.

Reuben Jackson
....

FOR THURMAN THOMAS

barely through
the second quarter—
and he has already
rushed through
swatches of
curses, blood
and astro turf
fourteen times—

a ballet of chalkboard
moves which sometimes
fail.

after the bodies rise,

he takes brief glimpses
at the sky,

and flags which seem
to point in the direction

of a quiet beach.

Elizabeth Alexander

....

TODAY'S NEWS

Heavyweight champion of the world Mike Tyson
broke his fist in a street brawl in Harlem
at three A.M. outside an all-night clothing store
where he was buying an 800-dollar, white
leather coat. The other dude, on TV, said,
"It was a sucker punch." Muhammad Ali said
Tyson ain't pretty enough to be heavyweight
champion of the world. Years ago a new Ali
threw his Olympic gold into the Ohio
River, said he'd get it when black people were truly
free in this country. In South Africa there is a dance
that says   we are fed up   we have no work   you have
struck a rock. I saw it on today's news.

I didn't want to write a poem that said "blackness
is," because we know better than anyone
that we are not one or ten or ten thousand things
Not one poem   We could count ourselves forever
and never agree on the number. When the first
black Olympic gymnast was black and on TV I called
home to say it was colored on channel three
in nineteen eighty-eight. Most mornings these days
Ralph Edwards comes into the bedroom and says, "Elizabeth,
this is your life. Get up and look for color,
look for color everywhere."

Robert Hayden

·········

[AMERICAN JOURNAL]

here among them   the americans   this baffling
multi people   extremes and variegations   their
noise   restlessness   their almost frightening
energy   how best describe these aliens in my
reports to The Counselors

disguise myself in order to study them unobserved
adapting their varied pigmentations   white black
red brown yellow   the imprecise and strangering
distinctions by which they live   by which they
justify their cruelties to one another

charming savages   enlightened primitives   brash
new comers lately sprung up in our galaxy   how
describe them   do they indeed know what or who
they are   do not seem to   yet no other beings
in the universe make more extravagant claims
for their importance and identity

like us they have created a veritable populace
of machines that serve and soothe and pamper
and entertain   we have seen their flags and
foot prints on the moon   also the intricate
rubbish left behind   a wastefully ingenious
people   many it appears worship the Unknowable
Essence   the same for them as for us   but are
more faithful to their machine made gods
technologists their shamans

oceans deserts mountains grain fields canyons
forests   variousness of landscapes weathers
sun light moon light as at home   much here is
beautiful   dream like vistas reminding me of
home   item   have seen the rock place known
as garden of the gods and sacred to the first
indigenes   red monoliths of home   despite
the tensions i breathe in i am attracted to
the vigorous americans   disturbing sensuous
appeal of so many   never to be admitted

something they call the american dream   sure
we still believe in it i guess   an earth man
in the tavern said   irregardless of the some
times night mare facts we always try to double
talk our way around   and its okay the dreams
okay and means whats good could be a damn sight
better   means every body in the good old u s a
should have the chance to get ahead or at least
should have three squares a day   as for myself
i do okay   not crying hunger with a loaf of
bread tucked under my arm you understand   i
fear one does not clearly follow i replied
notice you got a funny accent pal   like where
you from he asked   far from here i mumbled
he stared hard   i left

must be more careful   item   learn to use okay
their pass word   okay

crowds gathering in the streets today for some
reason obscure to me   noise and violent motion
repulsive physical contact   sentinels   pigs
i heard them called   with flailing clubs   rage
and bleeding and frenzy and screaming   machines
wailing   unbearable decibels   i fled lest
vibrations of the brutal scene do further harm
to my metabolism already over taxed

The Counselors would never permit such barbarous
confusion   they know what is best for our sereni
ty   we are an ancient race and have outgrown
illusions cherished here   item   their vaunted
liberty   no body pushes me around i have heard
them say   land of the free they sing   what do
they fear mistrust betray more than the freedom
they boast of in their ignorant pride   have seen
the squalid ghettoes in their violent cities
paradox on paradox   how have the americans
managed to survive

parades fireworks displays video spectacles
much grandiloquence much buying and selling
they are celebrating their history   earth men
in antique uniforms play at the carnage whereby
the americans achieved identity   we too recall
that struggle as enterprise of suffering and
faith uniquely theirs   blonde miss teen age
america waving from a red white and blue flower
float as the goddess of liberty   a divided
people seeking reassurance from a past few under
stand and many scorn   why should we sanction
old hypocrisies   thus dissenters   The Counse
lors would silence them

a decadent people The Counselors believe   i
do not find them decadent   a refutation not
permitted me   but for all their knowledge
power and inventiveness not yet more than raw
crude neophytes like earthlings everywhere

though i have easily passed for an american   in
bankers grey afro and dashiki long hair and jeans
hard hat yarmulke mini skirt   describe in some
detail for the amusement of The Counselors   and
though my skill in mimicry is impeccable   as
indeed The Counselors are aware   some thing
eludes me   some constant amid the variables
defies analysis and imitation   will i be judged
incompetent

america   as much a problem in metaphysics as
it is a nation earthly entity an iota in our
galaxy   an organism that changes even as i
examine it   fact and fantasy never twice the
same   so many variables

exert greater caution   twice have aroused
suspicion   returned to the ship until rumors
of humanoids from outer space   so their scoff
ing media voices termed us   had been laughed
away   my crew and i laughed too of course

confess i am curiously drawn   unmentionable   to
the americans   doubt i could exist among them for
long however   psychic demands far too severe
much violence   much that repels   i am attracted
none the less   their variousness their ingenuity
their elan vital   and that some thing   essence
quiddity   i cannot penetrate or name

TITLE INDEX

AUTHOR INDEX

I am grateful to all those noted below who granted me permission to reproduce their poems in this anthology. Special credit goes to Ahmos Zu-Bolton II, Eugene B. Redmond, Thomas Sayers Ellis, Joyce Rose, Roy McKay, and Jerry Ward, Jr., for helping me locate writers. Thanks also to Marie Brown, my agent, for opening the door. Many thanks for the wonderful women at Stewart, Tabori & Chang, some whose names are now biblical, Ann-Jeannette Campbell, Sarah Scheffel, Maureen Graney, and Alison Hagge, my editors. Thanks also to Jim Wageman, who created the design model for this book. Final thanks to Louise Ruck, Kathleen Baker, and Allison Bredlau of the English Department at the University of Nevada, Las Vegas, where I spent the Spring 1993 semester as a visiting professor and completed most of the work on this book.

POETRY CREDITS

ADESANYA ALAKOYE: "Eshu" is reprinted from *Tell Me How Willing Slaves Be* (Washington, D.C.: Energy BlackSouth Press, 1976) by permission of the publisher. ELIZABETH ALEXANDER: "Passage" and "Today's News" are reprinted from *The Venus Hottentot* (Charlottesville: University Press of Virginia, 1990) by permission of the University Press of Virginia. SAMUEL ALLEN: "To Satch" is reprinted from *First World* (vol. 1, no. 1, January/ February 1977). "Harriet Tubman Aka Moses" is reprinted from *American Negro Poetry*, edited by Arna Bontemps (New York: Hill & Wang, 1963). Both reprinted by permission of the author. MAYA ANGELOU: "Phenomenal Woman" and "Still I Rise" are reprinted from *And Still I Rise*, by Maya Angelou. Copyright © 1978 Maya Angelou. Reprinted by permission of Random House, Inc. Permission to publish in the United Kingdom and Canada granted by Virago Press Limited, London. ALVIN AUBERT: "The Opposite of Green" is reprinted from *Feeling Through: New Poems*, by Alvin Aubert (Greenfield Center, NY: Greenfield Review Press, 1975), by permission of the author. HOUSTON A. BAKER, JR.: "Toward Guinea: for Larry Neal, 1937-1981" is reprinted from *A Milestone Sampler: 15th Anniversary Anthology* (Detroit: Lotus Press, 1987) by permission of the author. AMINA BARAKA: "All Is One for Monk" is reprinted from *The Music: Reflections on Jazz and Blues*, edited by Amina Baraka and Amiri Baraka (New York: Morrow, 1987), by permission of the author. AMIRI BARAKA: a portion of "In the Tradition" is reprinted from *The Music: Reflections on Jazz and Blues*, by Amiri Baraka (LeRoi Jones) and Amina Baraka (New York: William Morrow, 1987). "Ka 'Ba" is reprinted from *New Black Voices* (New York: New American Library, 1972) by permission of the author. GEORGE BARLOW: "4½ Months: Halfway Song (Hey, Baby! What You Know Good?)" and "Mingus Speaks: Found Poems" are reprinted from *Gabriel* (Detroit: Broadside Press, 1974) by permission of the author. JONETTA BARRAS: "Peace" is reprinted from *Free D.C. (The Writers' Workshop)* (Washington, D.C.: Free D.C. Press, 1978) by permission of the author. GERALD BARRAX: "Strangers Like Us: Pittsburgh, Raleigh, 1945-1985" is reprinted from *Callaloo* (vol. 11, no. 3) by permission of Johns Hopkins University Press. SANDRA TURNER BOND: "Tuesday Night Affair" is reprinted from *Free D.C. (The Writers' Workshop)* (Washington, D.C.: Free D.C. Press, 1978) by permission of the author. GWENDOLYN BROOKS: "The Mother" is reprinted from *Blacks*, by Gwendolyn Brooks, copyright © 1991 Gwendolyn Brooks. "Primer for Blacks" is reprinted from *Primer for Blacks*, by Gwendolyn Brooks, copyright © 1991 Gwendolyn Brooks. Both books were published in 1991 by Third World Press, Chicago, IL. Both poems are reprinted by permission of the author. JAMES BROWN and ALFRED ELLIS: "Say It Loud—I'm Black and I'm Proud" © 1968 Dynatone Publishing Co. All rights administered by Unichappell Music Inc., Los Angeles, CA. All Rights Reserved. Used by permission. MELVIN E. BROWN: "Survival Motion: Notice" is reprinted from *In the First Place: Poems*, by Melvin E. Brown (Baltimore: Liberation House Press, 1974), by permission of the author. STERLING A. BROWN: "An Old Woman Remembers," "Ma Rainey," "Sister Lou," and "Strong Men" were reprinted from *The Collected Poems of Sterling A. Brown* by Sterling A. Brown. Copyright © 1980 Sterling A. Brown. Reprinted by permission of HarperCollins, Publishers, Inc. "An Old Woman Remembers" originally appeared in *Freedomways* (New York: Freedomways Associates). KENNETH CARROLL: "The Truth about Karen" is reprinted from *Something for My Sisters* (Washington,D.C.: Cuz on Bass Publishing, 1992) by permission of the author. PEARL CLEAGE: "Confession" is reprinted from *We Speak as Liberators*, edited by O. Coombs (New York: Dodd Mead, 1970), by permission of the author. LUCILLE CLIFTON: "I Am Accused of Tending to the Past," copyright © 1991 Lucille Clifton. Reprinted from *Quilting Poems 1987-1990*, by Lucille Clifton. "Good Times," "Listen Children," and "The Lost Baby Poem," copyright © 1987 Lucille Clifton. Reprinted from *Good Woman: Poems and a Memoir 1969-1980*, by Lucille Clifton. All reprinted by permission of BOA Editions, Ltd., 92 Park Ave., Brockport, NY 14420. MICHELLE T. CLINTON: "Eviction" is reprinted from *The Black Scholar* (vol. 19, nos. 4 & 5) by permission of the author. HORACE COLEMAN: "Poem for a 'Divorced' Daughter" is reprinted from *Between a Rock & a Hard Place* (Kansas City, MO: BkMk Press, 1977) by permission of the author. WANDA COLEMAN: "Coffee" is reprinted from *Mad Dog Black Lady* (Santa Barbara, CA: Black Sparrow Press, 1979) by permission of the author. JAYNE CORTEZ: All poems are copyright © 1993 Jayne Cortez and are reprinted by permission of the author. Poems originally appeared in slightly different versions in the following books. "How Long Has Trane Been Gone," *Pisstained Stairs and the Monkey Man's Wares* (New York: Phrase Text, 1969). "Pray for the

Lovers," *Festivals and Funerals* (New York: Phrase Text, 1971). "So Many Feathers," *Mouth on Paper* (New York: Bola Press, 1977). "Tapping," *Coagulations: New and Selected Poems* (New York: Thunder's Mouth Press, 1984). COUNTEE CULLEN: "Song in Spite of Myself" is reprinted from *The Black Christ and Some Poems,* by Countee Cullen. Copyright © 1929 by Harper & Brothers. Copyright © renewed 1957 by Ida M. Cullen. Permission granted by GRM Associates, Inc. WARING CUNEY: "No Images" is reprinted from Storefront Church, by William Waring Cuney (London: P. Breman, 1973), by permission by Paul Breman Limited. THULANI DAVIS: "Desire 1" and "Zoom (The Commodores)" are reprinted from *All the Renegade Ghosts Rise* (Washington, D.C.: Anemone Press, 1978) by permission of the author. TOM DENT: "For Cool Papa Bell" is reprinted from *Blue Lights and River Songs* (Detroit: Lotus Press, 1982) by permission of the author. TOI DERRICOTTE: "A Note on My Son's Face" is reprinted from *Callaloo* (vol. 10, no. 4) by permission of the author. MELVIN DIXON: "Places, Places" is reprinted from *Callaloo* (vol. 9, no. 1) by permission of Johns Hopkins University Press. OWEN DODSON: "Black Mother Praying" is reprinted from *Powerful Long Ladder* by Owen Dodson. Copyright © 1946 and renewed © 1974 by Owen Dodson. Reprinted by permission of Farrar, Straus & Giroux, Inc . THOMAS A. DORSEY: "Take My Hand, Precious Lord" © 1938 Unichappell Music Inc., Los Angeles, CA. (Renewed) All Rights Reserved. Used by Permission. RITA DOVE: "Adolescence — I," "Adolescence — II," and "Adolescence — III" are published by permission of the author. "Fifth Grade Autobiography" is reprinted from *Grace Notes,* by Rita Dove, with the permission of W. W. Norton & Company, Inc. Copyright © 1989 by Rita Dove. WILLIAM EDWARD BURGHARDT DU BOIS: "The Song of the Smoke" is reprinted from *Creative Writings by W. E. B. Du Bois: A Pageant, Poems, Short Stories and Playlets* (Kraus-Thomson Organization Limited, Millwood, NY, 1985) by permission of the Kraus Organization Limited. HENRY DUMAS: "Root Song" is reprinted from *Knees of a Natural Man,* edited by Eugene B. Redmond (New York: Thunder's Mouth Press, 1989). Copyright © 1969 - 1989 Loretta Dumas and Eugene B. Redmond. Used by permission. PAUL LAURENCE DUNBAR: "We Wear The Mask" and "When Malindy Sings" are reprinted from *The Collected Poetry of Paul Laurence Dunbar,* edited by Joanne Braxton (Charlottesville: University Press of Virginia, 1993). CORNELIUS EADY: "My Mother, If She Had Won Free Dance Lessons" is reprinted from *Kartunes* (West Orange, NJ: Warthog Press, 1980). "My Mother is a God Fearing Woman," and "Success" are reprinted from *Victims of the Latest Dance Craze: Poems,* by Cornelius Eady (Chicago: Ommation Press, 1986). All reprinted by permission of the author. MARI EVANS: "I Am a Black Woman" is reprinted from *I Am a Black Woman* (New York: William Morrow, 1979). "Who Can Be Born Black" is reprinted from *Nightstar* (Los Angeles: CAAS, University of California at Los Angeles, 1981). Both reprinted by permission of the author. NIKKY FINNEY: "Uncles" is reprinted from *On Wings Made of Gauze* (New York: Morrow, 1985) by permission of the author. ROBERT FLEMING: "For All Unwed Mothers" is reprinted from *Melons* (Cleveland: Melon Press, 1974) by permission of the author. CALVIN FORBES: "Picture of a Man" is published by permission of the author. RUTH GARNETT: "Dealing Scraps" is reprinted from *A Move Further South* (Chicago: Third World Press, 1987) by permission of the author. BRIAN G. GILMORE: "Bow to Allah" is published by permission of the author. NIKKI GIOVANNI: "Knoxville, Tennessee" and "Nikki-Rosa," © 1968, 1970 Nikki Giovanni are reprinted from *Black Feeling, Black Talk, Black Judgement.* "Ego Tripping (There May Be a Reason Why)" and "The Women Gather," © 1970, 1974, 1975 Nikki Giovanni are reprinted from *The Women and the Men.* All reprinted by permission of William Morrow & Company, Inc. FRANCES E. W.

HARPER: "The Slave Auction" and "Bury Me In A Free Land" are reprinted from *The Complete Poems of Frances E. W. Harper,* edited by Maryemma Graham. Copyright © 1988 Oxford University Press, Inc. Reprinted by permission. MICHAEL S. HARPER: "Alice," "Alone," "Breaded Meat, Breaded Hands," "Dear John, Dear Coltrane," and "Makin' Jump Shots" are reprinted from *Images of Kin* (Urbana: University of Illinois Press, 1977) by permission of the author. PETER HARRIS: "Some Songs Women Sing" is published by permission of the author. WILLIAM J. HARRIS: "A Daddy Poem" is reprinted from *Hey Fella Would You Mind Holding this Piano a Moment* (Greenfield Center, NY: Ithaca House, 1974) by permission of the author. ROBERT HAYDEN: "[American Journal]," "Runagate Runagate," "Frederick Douglass," and "Those Winter Sundays" are reprinted from *Collected Poems of Robert Hayden,* edited by Frederick Glaysher, by permission of Liveright Publishing Corporation. Copyright © 1985 Erma Hayden. SAFIYA HENDERSON-HOLMES : "Goodhousekeeping #17 (Kitchen Table)" is reprinted from *Madness and a Bit of Hope* (New York: Harlem River Press, 1990) by permission of the author. BELL HOOKS: "The Body inside the Soul" and "The Woman's Mourning Song" are reprinted from *The Woman's Mourning Song* (New York: Harlem River Press, 1993) by permission of the author. LANGSTON HUGHES: "Dream Variations," "Mother to Son," "The Negro Speaks of Rivers," and "The Weary Blues" are reprinted from *Selected Poems,* by Langston Hughes. Copyright © 1926 by Alfred A. Knopf, Inc. and renewed 1954 by Langston Hughes. Reprinted by permission of the publisher. "Feet O' Jesus" is reprinted from *The Dream Keeper and Other Poems,* by Langston Hughes. Copyright © 1927 by Alfred A. Knopf, Inc. and renewed 1955 by Langston Hughes. Reprinted by permission of the publisher. AKASHA (GLORIA) HULL: "Another Rhythm" is reprinted from *Healing Heart* (Latham, NY: Kitchen Table: Women of Color Press, 1989) by permission of the author. WELDON J. IRVINE, JR.: "To Be Young, Gifted and Black" by Nina Simone and Weldon J. Irvine, Jr. Copyright © 1969 EMI Grove Park Music, Inc., New York and Ninandy Music, Miami, FL. Rights for the U.S.A. and Canada controlled and administered jointly. Rights for the world administered by CPP/Belwin, Inc., Miami, FL. All rights reserved. ANGELA JACKSON: "Choosing the Blues" is reprinted from *The Black Scholar* (vol. 19, nos. 4 & 5) by permission of the author. REUBEN JACKSON: "For Thurman Thomas" is published by permission of the author. "Sunday Brunch" is reprinted from *Fingering the Keys* (Cabin John, MD: Gut Punch Press, 1990) by permission of the author. HARRIET JACOBS: "It Is Not Just" and "On Growing Up the Darker Berry" are published by permission of the author. LANCE JEFFERS: "My Blackness is the Beauty of this Land" and "When I Know the Power of My Black Hand" are reprinted by permission of the Broadside Press. GEORGIA DOUGLAS JOHNSON: "The Heart of a Woman" and "I Want to Die While You Love Me" are reprinted from *Black Sister: Poetry by Black American Women,* edited by Erlene Stetson (Bloomington: Indiana University Press, 1981). JAMES WELDON JOHNSON: "The Creation" and "Go Down Death" are reprinted from *God's Trombones* by James Weldon Johnson. Copyright © 1927 The Viking Press, Inc., renewed © 1955 by Grace Nail Johnson. "Lift Every Voice and Sing" and "Sence You Went Away" are reprinted from *Saint Peter Relates an Incident* by James Weldon Johnson. Copyright © 1917, 1921, 1935 by James Weldon Johnson, copyright renewed © 1963 by Grace Nail Johnson. All used by permission of Viking Penguin, a division of Penguin Books USA, Inc. JACQUIE JONES: "Drugs" is reprinted from *Callaloo* (vol. 13, no. 2) by permission of the author. PATRICIA JONES: "Song" is reprinted from *Women Surviving Massacres and Men: Nine Women Poets, An Anthology,* edited by E. Ethelbert Miller (Washington, D.C.: Anemone Press, 1977) by permission of the author. JUNE

JORDAN: "Grand Army Plaza," "Poem about My Rights," and "The Test of Atlanta 1979—" are reprinted from *Passion: New Poems, 1977-1980*, by June Jordan (Boston: Beacon Press, 1980). "Poem Against the State (of Things): 1975" is reprinted from *Things I Do in the Dark: Selected Poetry*, by June Jordan (New York: Random House, 1977). All reprinted by permission of the author. NORMAN JORDAN: "When a Woman Gets Blue" is reprinted from *Destination Ashes*, by Norman Jordan (Chicago: Third World Press, 1970), by permission of the author. BOB KAUFMAN: "Battle Report" is reprinted from *Solitude Crowded with Loneliness*, by Bob Kaufman. Copyright © 1965 by Bob Kaufman. "Private Sadness" and "Untitled" are reprinted from *The Ancient Rain* by Bob Kaufman. Copyright © 1981 by Bob Kaufman. All reprinted by permission of New Directions Publishing Corp. DOLORES KENDRICK "Sidney, Looking for Her Mother…" is reprinted from *The Women of Plums* (New York: Morrow, 1989) by permission of the author. ETHERIDGE KNIGHT: "As You Leave Me," "The Idea of Ancestry," and "To Make a Poem in Prison" are reprinted from *The Essential Etheridge Knight*, by Etheridge Knight, by permission of the University of Pittsburgh Press. Copyright © 1986 Etheridge Knight. YUSEF KOMUNYAKAA: "Slam, Dunk, & Hook" is reprinted from *Magic City* © 1992 Yusef Komunyakaa, Wesleyan University Press, by permission of University Press of New England. "Boxing Day," "My Father's Loveletters," and "White Port and Lemon Juice" are published by permission of the author. PINKIE GORDON LANE: "Rain Ditch" is reprinted from *Literati Internazaionale* (vol. 1, no. 1, 1991) by permission of the author. ELOUISE LOFTIN: "Weeksville Women" is reprinted from *Jumbish*, by Elouise Loftin (New York: Emerson Hall Publishers, 1972), by permission of the author. Copyright © Elouise Loftin, 1972. AUDRE LORDE: "Between Ourselves" is reprinted from *The Black Unicorn, Poems by Audre Lorde*, by permission of W. W. Norton & Company, Inc. Copyright © 1978 Audre Lorde. Permission to publish in the United Kingdom granted by Charlotte Sheedy Literary Agency, Inc., New York. "Naturally" is reprinted from *New York Head Shop and Museum*, by Audre Lorde (Detroit: Broadside Press, 1975), by permission of the publisher. MONIFA ATUNGAYE LOVE: "Initiation" is reprinted from *Provisions: Poems*, by Monifa Atungaye (Detroit: Lotus Press, 1989), by permission of the author. COLLEEN J. MCELROY: "Illusion" is reprinted from *Winters Without Snow* (New York: I. Reed Books, 1979) by permission of the author. CLAUDE MCKAY: "The Harlem Dancer," "If We Must Die," and "The White House" are reprinted from *Selected Poems of Claude McKay*, published by Harcourt Brace. Permission is granted by The Archives of Claude McKay, Carl Crowl, Administrator. NAOMI LONG MADGETT: "Black Woman" is reprinted from *Black Sister: Poetry by Black American Women*, edited by Erlene Stetson (Bloomington, IN: Indiana University Press, 1981), by permission of the author. HAKI R. MADHUBUTI: "My Brothers" is reprinted from *Earthquake and Sunrise Missions* (Chicago: Third World Press, 1983). "A Poem Looking for a Reader," is reprinted from *Don't Cry, Scream*, by Don L. Lee (Detroit: Broadside Press, 1969), "The Union of Two" is reprinted from *Killing Memory, Seeking Ancestors*, by Haki R. Madhubuti (Detroit: Lotus Press, 1987). All reprinted by permission of the author. LAINI MATAKA: "Next Door" and "Ornithology" are reprinted from *Never As Strangers* (Baltimore: W. M. Duforcelf, 1988) by permission of the author. E. ETHELBERT MILLER: "Another Love Affair/Another Poem" is reprinted from *Where Are the Love Poems for Dictators?* (Seattle: Open Hand, 1986). "Rebecca" is reprinted from *First Light* (Baltimore: Black Classic Press, 1994). "Tomorrow" is reprinted from *Seasons of Hunger/Cry of Rain* (Detroit: Lotus Press, 1982). All reprinted by permission of the author. MAY MILLER: "A Closing" is reprinted from *The Ransomed Wait*, by May Miller (Detroit: Lotus Press, 1983), by permission of Lotus Press. LENARD D. MOORE: "A

Bluesman's Blues" is reprinted from *Callaloo* (vol. 14, no. 4) by permission of the author. "Winter 1967" is published by permission of the author. GEORGE MOSBY, JR.: "To Josh Gibson (Legendary Slugger of the Old Negro Baseball League)" is reprinted from *Population* (Brooklyn: Hanging Loose Press, 1983) by permission of Hanging Loose Press. HARRYETTE MULLEN: "The Dance She Does," "Momma Sayings," "Roadmap," and "Saturday Afternoon, When Chores are Done" are reprinted from *Tree Tall Woman* (Galveston, TX: Energy Earth Communications, 1981) by permission of the author. LARRY NEAL: "Don't Say Goodbye to the Pork-Pie Hat" is reprinted from *Hoodoo Hollerin' Bebop Ghosts*, by Larry Neal. Copyright © 1968, 1974 Larry Neal. Reprinted by permission of Howard Univesity Press. MICHELLE PARKERSON: "Statistic" is published by permission of the author. PUBLIC ENEMY (C. Ridenhow/H. Shocklee/E. Sadler): "Party for Your Right to Fight" © 1988 Def American Songs, Inc., New York and Bring the Noize, Inc., New York. Used with permission. DUDLEY RANDALL: "Ballad of Birmingham" is reprinted from *Poem Counterpoem*, by Dudley Randall and Margaret Danner, copyright © 1969. Reprinted by permission of Broadside Press. "Blackberry Sweet" is reprinted from *New Black Poetry*, edited by Clarence Major (New York: International Publishers, 1969), by permission of Broadside Press. EUGENE B. REDMOND: "Dance Bodies #1," "Love Necessitates," "My Tongue Paints a Path," and "Poetic Reflections Enroute to, and During, the Funeral and Burial of Henry Dumas, Poet" are published by permission of the author. ISHMAEL REED: "The Black Cock" and "White Hope" are reprinted from *New Collected Poems*, by Ishmael Reed. Copyright © 1972 Ishmael Reed. Reprinted by permission of Atheneum Publishers, an imprint of Macmillan Publishing Company. Permission to publish in the United Kingdom and Canada granted by Whitman & Ransom. PRIMUS ST. JOHN: "Lynching and Burning" is reprinted from *Skins on the Earth*, by Primus St. John (Port Townsend, WA: Copper Canyon Press, 1975). "Sunday" is reprinted from *Dreamer* (Pittsburgh: Carnegie-Mellon University Press, 1990). Both reprinted by permission of the author. CAROLYN RODGERS: "Group Therapy," "Poem No. 1," and "Slave Ritual" are reprinted from *The Heart as Ever Green*, by Carolyn M. Rodgers. Copyright © 1978 Carolyn Rodgers. Reprinted by permission of Doubleday, a division of Bantam Doubleday Dell Publishing Group, Inc. KALAMU YA SALAAM: "Our World Is Less Full Now That Mr. Fuller Is Gone" is reprinted from *Nommo: a Literary Legacy of Black Chicago (1967-1987), Authors of the Obac Writers Workshop*, edited by Carole A. Parks (New York: OBAhouse, 1987), by permission of the author. SONIA SANCHEZ: "Haiku" is reprinted from *Under a Soprano Sky*, by Sonia Sanchez (Trenton, NJ: Africa World Press, Inc., 1987). "Right On: White America" is reprinted from *The Poetry of Black America: Anthology of the 20th Century*, edited by Arnold Adoff (New York: Harper & Row, 1973). "To Anita" is reprinted from *BlackSpirit: a Festival of New Black Poets in America*, edited by Woodie King (New York: Random House, 1972). All reprinted by permission of the author. GIL SCOTT-HERON: "Winter in America" is reprinted from *So Far, So Good*, by Gil Scott-Heron (Chicago: Third World Press, 1990), by permission of Third World Press. TIM SEIBLES: "Who" is reprinted from *Body Moves* (San Antonio, TX: Corona Publishing Company, 1988) by permission of the author. NTOZAKE SHANGE: "About Atlanta" and "You Are Sucha Fool" are reprinted from *A Daughter's Geography*, by Ntozake Shange. Copyright © 1984 Ntozake Shange. "My Father Is a Retired Magician," "I Live in Music," and "Where the Mississippi Meets the Amazon" are reprinted from *Nappy Edges*, by Ntozake Shange. Copyright © 1972, 1974, 1975, 1976, 1977, 1978 Ntozake Shange. All reprinted with permission from St. Martin's Press, Inc., New York, NY. Permission to publish in the United Kingdom is granted by Russell & Volkening, New York.

CHARLOTTE WATSON SHERMAN: "Roots" is reprinted from *Gathering Ground*, edited by Jo Cochran, J. T. Stewart, and Mayumi Tsutakawa (Seattle, WA: Seal Press, 1984), by permission of the author. SHARYN JEANNE SKEETER: "Midwest, Midcentury," "California, 1852," and "Western Trail Cook, 1880" are published by permission of the author. A. B. SPELLMAN: "The Twist" is reprinted from *The Beautiful Days* (New York: The Poets Press, 1965). "When Black People Are" is reprinted from *The Poetry of Black America: Anthology of the 20th Century*, edited by Arnold Adoff (New York: Harper & Row, 1973). Both reprinted by permission of the author. LAMONT B. STEPTOE: "O' Yes" is reprinted from *American Morning/Mourning* (Camden, NJ: Whirlwind Press, 1990) by permission of the author. SHARAN STRANGE: "Barbershop Ritual" is reprinted from *Callaloo* (vol. 14, no. 2, 1991) by permission of Johns Hopkins University Press. NATASHA TARPLEY: "Feel Free" is published by permission of the author. GARTH TATE: "Last Instructions" is published by permission of the poet's family. GREG S. TATE: "Tonguing" is reprinted from *Free D.C. (The Writers' Workshop)* (Washington, D.C.: Free D.C. Press, 1978) by permission of the author. JEAN TOOMER: "Song of the Son" is reprinted from *Cane*, by Jean Toomer, by permission of Liveright Publishing Corporation. Copyright © 1923 Boni & Liveright. Copyright renewed © 1951 by Jean Toomer. ASKIA M. TOURE: "The Frontier of Rage" is reprinted from *The Pyramids to the Projects* (Trenton, NJ: Africa World Press, 1990) by permission of the author. NANCY TRAVIS: "At My Father's House," "Church Ladies," and "Sunbathing" are reprinted from *April + June* (Berkeley: Shameless Hussy Press, 1987) by permission of the author. QUINCY TROUPE: "Conjuring against Alien Spirits" and "A Poem for Magic" are reprinted from *Weather Reports: New and Selected Poems* (New York: Harlem River Press, 1991), by permission of the author. VEGA: "Brothers Loving Brothers" is reprinted from *Brother to Brother: New Writings by Black Gay Men*, edited by Essex Hemphill (Boston, MA: Alyson Publications, 1991) by permission of the author. PAUL VESEY: see Samuel Allen. GLORIA WADE-GAYLES: "Inquisition" and "Loving Again" are reprinted from *Anointed to Fly* (New York: Harlem River Press, 1991) by permission of the author. ALICE WALKER: "Did This Happen to Your Mother? Did Your Sister Throw Up a Lot?," copyright © 1979 Alice Walker, and "Good Night, Willie Lee, I'll See You in the Morning," copyright © 1975 Alice Walker, are reprinted from *Good Night, Willie Lee, I'll See You in the Morning: Poems,* by Alice Walker (New York: Dial Press, 1979), by permission of Doubleday, a division of Bantam Doubleday Dell Publishing Group, Inc. Permission to publish in the United Kingdom granted by David Higham Associates, London. MARGARET WALKER: "For My People" is reprinted from *This is My Century: New and Collected Poems* (Athens: University of Georgia Press, 1989) by permission of The University of Georgia Press. MARILYN NELSON WANIEK: "Bali Hai Calls Mama" and "Sleepness Nights" are reprinted from *Mama's Promises: Poems*, by Marilyn Nelson Waniek (Baton Rouge: Louisiana State University Press, 1985), by permission of Louisiana State University Press. Copyright © 1985 Marilyn Nelson Waniek. JERRY W. WARD, JR.: "Comfort-Maker" is reprinted from *The Black Scholar* (Fall 1988, Black World Foundation, San Francisco, CA) by permission of the author. MICHAEL S. WEAVER: "The Picnic, an Homage to Civil Rights" is reprinted from *Callaloo*, (vol. 12, no. 3,) by permission of the author and the Johns Hopkins University Press. "Water Song" is reprinted from *Water Song*, by Michael S. Weaver (Lexington: University of Kentucky, 1985), by permission of the author. PHILLIS WHEATLEY: "On Being Brought from Africa to America" is reprinted from *The Complete Works of Phillis Wheatley*, edited by John C. Shields. Copyright © 1988 Oxford University Press, Inc. Reprinted by permission. JAY WRIGHT: "Wednesday Night Prayer Meeting" is reprinted from *The Home Coming Singer* (New York: Corinth Books, 1971) by permission of the author. RICHARD WRIGHT: "Between the World and Me" is reprinted from *R. W. Reader*, (New York: Doubleday, 1935) by permission of John Hawkins & Associates, Inc. Copyright © 1935 Richard Wright. STEPHEN CALDWELL WRIGHT: "Out of the Wailing" is reprinted from *Out of the Wailing*, by Stephen Caldwell Wright (Longwood, FL: Christopher-Burghardt Associates, 1992), by permission of the author. AL YOUNG: "A Dance for Ma Rainy," copyright © 1968 Al Young, is reprinted from *Dancing*, by Al Young (New York: Corinth Books, 1969), by permission of the author. KEVIN YOUNG: "Eddie Priest's Barber Shop & Notary: Closed Mondays" is reprinted from *Calalloo* (vol. 14, no. 4) by permission of the author. AHMOS ZU-BOLTON II: "Struggle-Road Dance" is reprinted from *First World* (vol. 1, no. 1) by permission of the author.

Every effort has been made to trace copyright holders. Stewart, Tabori & Chang would be interested in hearing from any copyright holders not here acknowledged.

The type in this book was set in
Lithos for headings
Adobe Garamond for text

Old style figures and small caps were set in
Adobe Garamond Expert

The book was printed by
Quebecor Printing, Eusey Press
Leominster, Massachusetts
and bound by
Quebecor Printing, Book Press
Brattleboro, Vermont